THE DHARMADHĀTUSTAVA

CRITICALLY EDITED

BY

LIU ZHEN

CHINA TIBETOLOGY RESEARCH CENTER
AUSTRIAN ACADEMY OF SCIENCES
ASIA-AFRICA INSTITUTE (UNIVERSITY OF HAMBURG)

Sanskrit Texts from the Tibetan Autonomous Region

founded by

Lhagpa Phuntshogs and **Ernst Steinkellner**

edited in chief by

Dramdul, Ernst Steinkellner, Harunaga Isaacson

No.17

中国藏学研究中心
奥地利科学院
德国汉堡大学亚非研究所

西藏自治区梵文文本系列丛书

创办人
拉巴平措 与 恩斯特· 斯坦因凯勒

主编
郑堆，恩斯特· 斯坦因凯勒，春永· 艾萨克森

第十七卷

CHINA TIBETOLOGY RESEARCH CENTRE
AUSTRIAN ACADEMY OF SCIENCES

The Dharmadhātustava

A Critical Edition of the Sanskrit Text with the Tibetan and Chinese Translations, a Diplomatic Transliteration of the Manuscript and Notes

by

Liu Zhen

CHINA TIBETOLOGY PUBLISHING HOUSE

AUSTRIAN ACADEMY OF SCIENCES PRESS

BEIJING – VIENNA 2015

Submitted to the Austrian Academy of Sciences

on May 4th, 2014

by Ernst Steinkellner, member of the Academy

ISBN 978-3-7001-7764-7

Printed by Peking Longchang Weiye Print Ltd.

Contents

Acknowledgments **vii**

Introduction **ix**

Conventions and Abbreviations **xxxiii**

Diplomatic Edition **1**

Critical Edition **7**

Critical Edition of Tibetan Text **29**

Critical Edition of Chinese Texts **47**

Appendix: Diplomatic Edition of Some Unknown Text(s) which bear(s) a Title *Pañcarakṣāhṛdaya-bījamantra* according to Luo Zhao's Catalogue **69**

Pāda Index **76**

Bibliography **87**

Acknowledgments

It was in the autumn of 2005 that I first encountered the Sanskrit text of the *Dharmadhātustava*, ascribed to Nāgārjuna. My doctoral supervisor, Professor Jens-Uwe Hartmann (Munich), offered me a copy of this text (originally from Professor Ernst Steinkellner in Vienna) as material for a proposed topic for my dissertation. Unfortunately, due to several unforeseen reasons, I did not undertake the editing of this text at that time. Instead, I took on another task to which I thoroughly dedicated myself, finishing my doctorate in 2008.

Notwithstanding, the first eight stanzas on the first page of that *Dharmadhātustava* manuscript, which I already started to transliterate and translate at that time, had left a deep impression on me and ignited a glowing longing to resume work on the entire text. A year after finishing my doctorate, Dr. Johannes Schneider (Munich), who had initiated me into the knowledge of Sanskrit at the beginning of my studies in Indology and who has remained a dear friend over all these years, guided me to embark on yet another wondrous project. He recommended that I ask the Institute for the Culture and Intellectual History of Asia (IKGA) of the Austrian Academy of Sciences directly for permission to continue the editing of the *Dharmadhātustava* manuscript.

The former director of the IKGA, Professor Ernst Steinkellner, and his successor Dr. Helmut Krasser, who passed away only several months ago, kindly approved this proposal and incorporated it into the framework of the series *Sanskrit Texts from the Tibetan Autonomous Region*. Over the last years, I have received many invaluable suggestions and comments from them on my work, for which I am very grateful.

In addition, it would have been impossible to complete the present work without the precious help of the following colleagues: Professor Harunaga Isaacson (Hamburg), Professor Kazuo Kano (Koyasan), Professor Seishi Karashima (Tokyo), Professor Guoliang Lin (Shanghai), Professor Jonathan Silk (Leiden), Dr. Gergely Hidas, Dr. Peter Szántó (Oxford), and the two anonymous reviewers of my draft, who all offered me various pieces of advice, including corrections of my readings and interpretation; Mr. Tao Pan (Munich) and Ms. Cynthia Peck-Kubaczek (Vienna), who edited and improved my English; Dr. Anne MacDonald (Vienna), who tirelessly checked my text as well as my English; and Ms. Linkun Gong (Shanghai), who provided me with technical support during the preparation of the layout. My particular thanks are also due to Professor Francesco Sferra (Naples), who dedicated a large amount of his time to the reading of my drafts together with me, side by side and again and again.

Last but not least, I would like to express my heartfelt thanks to my "*Doktorvater*," Professor Hartmann, for having once again taken part in supervising this work, which still reminds me of the beautiful time I spent in Munich while working on my M.A. thesis and doctoral dissertation.

Finally, I would like to mention the following institutions with due appreciation: The China Tibetology Research Center and the IKGA, which together initiated and permitted me to embark on this project, with the latter also kindly providing me accommodation during my sojourns in Vienna; and the Fudan University Humanities Fund Project and the 985 III Project, which provided the funding that enabled me to complete this research.

Introduction

1. General remarks

Although the *Dharmadhātustava*[1] (DDhS) has been ascribed to Nāgārjuna,[2] this attribution has been questioned by TSUKINOWA (1934) and SEYFORT RUEGG (1971: 453-54) and rejected by LINDTNER (1982: 10).[3] Judging from its style and content, which shows significant influence from the *tathāgatagarbha*-tradition, the author of the DDhS cannot be the same as that of the *Mūlamadhyamakakārikā*. Another possible indication for the non-authenticity of this work is the fact that we do not find any Indian commentaries on it.[4]

Nevertheless, great significance has been attached to the DDhS in the Indo-Tibetan Tantric tradition. Bhāviveka,[5]

---

[1] Both forms, *Dharmadhātu-stava* and *-stotra*, are attested as the title of this text, cf. SEYFORT RUEGG 1971: 448, n. 1 and HAYASHIMA 1987: 41. Following the majority of the scholars who have studied this text, the former form of its title, *Dharmadhātustava*, is used in this edition.

[2] It has been brought to our attention that Lobsang Dorjee (Sarnath) and Drasko Mitrikeski (Sydney) are also working on the Sanskrit text of the *Dharmadhātustava*.

[3] In addition to SEYFORT RUEGG 1971, other works investigating the DDhS include: TSUKINOWA 1933, 1934, HAYASHIMA 1987, BRUNNHÖLZL 2007 and MOCHIZUKI 2008. However, since the Sanskrit text was regarded as lost, it was not taken into account in any of the studies published to date.

[4] Cf. BRUNNHÖLZL 2007: 130.

[5] A quotation is found in the *Madhyamakaratnapradīpa*; cf. BRUNNHÖLZL 2007: 130. According to SEYFORT RUEGG 1990 (59-71) and KRASSER 2011 (231, n. 100), the author of this work is the second Bhāviveka, who lived after the sixth-century author of the *Madhyamakahṛdayakārikā* and the *Prajñāpradīpamūlamadhyamakavṛtti*. See the discussion on the authorship of the *Madhyamakaratnapradīpa* in ECKEL 2008: 23-27.

Nāropā,[6] Ratnākaraśānti, Dharmendra, Atiśa, etc., as well as a large number of Tibetan authors cite stanzas from the DDhS and clearly ascribe authority to it. Upon its introduction into Tibet, numerous commentaries were written on it by the local Tibetan masters, most of whom were Sakyapa or non-Gelugpa.[7]

2. Source materials

The source materials for this edition are: a Sanskrit Ms found in Tibet, the Tibetan translation by Kṛṣṇa Paṇḍita and Nag tsho lo tsā ba Tshul khrims rgyal ba[8] dated to the middle of the eleventh century, and three Chinese translations, the first undertaken by 不空金剛 (Amoghavajra) in about A.D. 765 (henceforth: Ch1),[9] the second by 施護 (*Dānapāla or *Dānarakṣita) between A.D. 1015 and 1019 (henceforth: Ch2),[10] and the third, the earliest but of doubtful authority, by 室利末多 (*Śrīmadda) in A.D. 707.[11]

---

[6] In his *Sekoddeśaṭīkā* (*Paramārthasaṃgraha*, SUṬ), six stanzas (18-23) of the DDhS are cited, which provide the only other Sanskrit evidence for the work; the other known quotations are in Tibetan. With the exception of one word in 18d and various scribal slips in the *Sekoddeśaṭīkā* Mss' citations, the Sanskrit quotations match up almost perfectly with the corresponding verses of the DDhS. Cf. the edition of SUṬ in CARELLI 1941: 66 and SFERRA & MERZAGORA 2006: 188, and the quotion in SEYFORT RUEGG 1971: 466, n. 82.

[7] Cf. BRUNNHÖLZL 2007: 130-152.

[8] Cf. the colophon of T and SEYFORT RUEGG 1971: 463 and n. 68.

[9] TSUKINOWA 1934: 425 and CHOU 1945: 296.

[10] He and two Indian monks led a project to translate 大教王經 (**Sarvatathāgatatattvasaṃgrahasūtra*), during which this later Chinese version of the DDhS must have been made. Cf. TSUKINOWA 1934: 419. It is worth remarking that all the translators of the three translations, T, Ch1 and Ch2, had a tantric background.

[11] Cf. § 2.3.

2.1. The Sanskrit manuscript

2.1.1. Description

The present work is based on two pages of black-and-white photocopies of a Ms whose original is kept in the Potala. They show, respectively, the *recto* and *verso* of eight folios as well as a numbering label. This label bears the following information in Chinese and Tibetan: "*źwa lu*, number 53, number of folios: 8." This indicates that the Ms came from Żalu, TAR. By means of the label, these eight folios can be identified with a Ms listed in Luo Zhao's catalogue,[12] namely, the sixth text listed under the Ms "Potala, Tanjur, item no. 8." Luo Zhao notes: "The Sūtras, *Pañcarakṣāhṛdayabījamantraḥ* (*sic*), etc., are in one bundle with a label, 'Źalu, No. 53, eight folios'. Three folios deal with the *Pañcarakṣāhṛdayabījamantra*, measuring 30.5 by 4.3 cm, black ink, Dhārikā script, 4-5 lines. The other five folios concern some kind of *stava*, without title, with its beginning and end, measuring 30.5 by 4.4 cm, black ink, Dhārikā script, 5 lines." The copy of this collective Ms is now kept in the CTRC's library, Box Nr. 185, item 6.

The five folios of the unnamed *stava*, which are represented as the first five folios on each photocopy, contain nothing other than the DDhS. Contrary to Luo Zhao's assessment, the last folio of the work is missing.[13] His comment, however, that the *Pañcarakṣāhṛdayabījamantra*, whose rectos and versos are also found on our copies, is contained in

[12] For Luo Zhao's catalogue, cf. STEINKELLNER 2007: xii, n. 5.

[13] It is possible that the seventh Ms listed under the same heading in Luo Zhao's catalogue is the missing end of the DDhS, but in another form (different size, script, etc.). He states: "Some kind of *stava*, one folio, with a label 'Źalu, No. 51, one folio', palm leaf, measuring 26.1 by 4.6 cm, black ink, Gupta script, 6 lines." If this folio indeed contains the end of the DDhS, it could be a remnant of an earlier copy, of which the preceding five-sixths of the text would have been replaced by the five folios listed as Źalu, No. 53.

three folios is correct, although he does not mention the additional material contained in them.[14]

The five DDhS Ms folios are paginated with the numerals 1-5 in the left margins of the *recto*s. Each folio contains five lines, except for the left part of folio 4a, which has six lines. Each line contains from 51 to 57 *akṣara*s, with a few exceptions (50 *akṣara*s in 2b5, 58 in 4b4, 59 in 5a3, only 23 in 2a5, 20 in 4a6 and 37 in 5b5). Each folio has a string-hole in the left half, at about a third of the way into the folio. The hole is located in the third line in a vertical oblong space that interrupts the lines and is 3-4 *akṣara*s in width. The left edges of folios 3 and 4 have been damaged by insects or worms, but the text has not been affected much. Judging from the photocopy, the quality of the original is only diminished by occasional fading or blotting.

The Ms is written in old Nepālī[15] script which, based on BÜHLER (1896: Tafel VI, column XV), BENDALL (1992: plate IV, Add. 866, 1643 and 1684) and MACDONALD (2005: ix-xxii), would appear to date to the eleventh century. It might be noted that certain *akṣara*s, like *e*, *tha*, *dha*, *bha* and *gha*, preserve their older forms (forms that started to disappear after the eleventh century), while some *akṣara*s, like *kha*, *pha*, *la* and *śa*, appear in more developed forms, i.e., those that would predominate in later centuries. Initial *e*  (2a3) appears in its archaic closed form. For comparison with its developed form see MACDONALD 2005;[16] see *e* of Mss dated 857 (Add. 1049) and 1008 (Add. 866) as found in Bendall's Table of Letters. *tha*  (3a2) and *dha*  (1a1), with respec-

[14] Actually, in addition to the *Pañcarakṣāhṛdayabījamantra*, the three folios bear a colophon, other mantras and a series of verses used in everyday ritual; cf. the diplomatic edition in Appendix. The preserved colophon indicates that these three folios were written during Kings Lakṣmīkāmadeva and Rudradeva's shared reign of Nepal. According to PETECH (1984: 35-39), this must have occurred between A.D. 1010 and 1028.

[15] For reasons for designating the script Nepālī instead of Nevārī, cf. Iain Sinclair's explanation under: http://www.danielstender.com/granthinam/1373/#respond.

[16] MACDONALD 2005: xix ff. and n. 19.

tively open tops, are almost the same except that *tha* has a middle horizontal line, and *dha* a pointed bottom. However, in rare cases *tha*  (2a5) has a still more pointed bottom. *Bha*  (4b4) occurs in its older form, which lacks a curved stroke extending to the right beneath the left part of the *akṣara*, as seen in the developed form. *gha*  (1a3) is in its older form; see the *gha* in BÜHLER's Tafel VI, 18 and BENDALL's plate IV. *kha*  (4b1) in our Ms represents a development of the older form. *pha*  (1b4) is similar to the modern form. *la*  (1a5) has a full right vertical stroke; in other eleventh century forms it often does not.[17] *śa*  (5b1) appears in a more developed form.[18]

It should be noted that the other three folios which have been included with the Ms of the DDhS have been copied by another scribe.[19] However, the two Mss are almost in the same style, and can both be dated to the same period, namely the beginning of the eleventh century.[20]

The orthography has the following characteristics: a) alternating use of *s*, *ṣ*, *ś*, b) non-differentiation of *v* and *b*, c) occasional alternation of *kṣ* and *k*, and of *kṣy* and *ky*, d) reduction of the double consonant in *ttva* to *t*, e) gemination of consonants after the semi-vowel *r*, albeit not consistently, f) occasional alternation of *n* and *ṇ*, g) lack of *avagraha*, h) occasional alternation of *ddh*, *dv* and *db* (2b3, *pratyātmayogitvād buddhāṇāṃ* and 2b4, *govidvānaṃ*).

Errors occur frequently due to the similarity of certain *akṣara*s; for example, *p* and *ṣ* (1b3, *ṣrabhāvyate* for *prab-*

---

17 Cf. BÜHLER 1896: Tafel VI, 42.

18 According to Bendall (1992: xxv), this form is attested only in a Ms dated 1065. However, the DDhS Ms is probably earlier than this Ms; cf. n. 14.

19 Characteristics of this scribe that distinguish him from the one who copied the DDhS: a thicker end of the downward curve in *ru*, *tha* and *dha* sometimes written with closed tops (however less frequently than open tops), *na* and *ra* in a slightly more hooked style, etc.

20 The basis of the paleographic analysis and the fact that the eight folios were bundled together, it cannot entirely be ruled out that the colophon (see n. 14) found on one of the three folios with the *Pañcarakṣāhṛdayabījamantra* was intended to belong to both the *Pañcarakṣāhṛdayabījamantra* and the DDhS.

hāvyate;[21] 2b1, *strīṣuṃstvaṃ* for *strīpuṃstvaṃ*; 4a5, *bodhiṣuṣṭir* for *bodhipuṣṭir*); *y* and *ṣ* (5a2, *durjaṣānā* for *durjayānā*; 5a2, *sudurjaṣā* for *sudurjayā*); and due to the random elision of *anusvāra*, the overlooking of several *pāda*s (4b1, <69d-71a>[22]), etc. The use of *daṇḍa* and double-*daṇḍa* is not always in accord with the metrical requirements. The places where insertions are to be made are marked in the text with upward- or downward-pointing *kākapada*s. The *akṣara*s to be inserted are found in the top or bottom margins of the Ms.

The language of the text is classical Sanskrit,[23] with the exception of one single word, *kaḍevare* (3b4, <48a>) instead of *kalevare*,[24] and one single form, *jñānārciṣaiḥ* (5a1-2, <71c>) instead of *jñānārcirbhiḥ*,[25] which may be Middle Indic.[26].

If we count the six *pāda*s missing in the Ms (but found in all translations) from the end of f. 4a and the beginning of f. 4b, the Ms ends at the beginning of *pāda* 86c. As we know that T has a total of 101 verses and approximately eight stanzas occupy one side of the folios of our Sanskrit Ms, the last 15 verses and a possible colophon would have filled one more complete folio.

The metre of the text is *anuṣṭubh* with *vipulā*s in 40c, 71c (*na-vipulā*), 37c (*bha-vipulā*), 2a, 9c, 15a, 22c,[27] 25c,[28]

---

[21] Which is then corrected to *prabhāsate*.

[22] The stanza numberings of different texts are placed in brackets of different shape; cf. below, Conventions *b*.

[23] Remarkably, there is a word, *ghaṭa*, whose gender is normally masculine and here neuter, cf. 6b and 7b.

[24] Cf. BHSD: *s.v. kaḍevara*, CPD and EWAia: *s.v. kaḷebara*.

[25] Cf. BHSG: § 16.36.

[26] There is still one more word, *ārūpam* (3a4, <40b>) instead of *ārūpyam*, which may be Buddhist Hybrid Sanskrit, cf. BHSD: *s.v. ārūpa*. Since *ārūpya* is an abstract form of *arūpa*, and the latter brings minimal change to the critical edition, the Ms.'s. *ārūpam* has been emended to *arūpam*.

[27] With an error in the 3rd syllable.

[28] With an error in the 4th syllable.

27a, 49a, 51a,[29] 56c (*ma-vipulā*), 45c,[30] 49c and 59a[31] (*ra-vipulā*).[32]

If some (not strictly speaking) rhyming was intended, it resulted in an awkward imitation of an *alaṃkāra*, i.e., *yamaka*, for example:

ya eva dhātuḥ saṃsāre
śodhyamānaḥ **sa eva** tu |
śuddhaḥ **sa eva** nirvāṇe
dharmakāyaḥ **sa eva** hi || <2>

ya**thā hi** kṣīra**sammiśraṃ**
sarpimaṇḍaṃ **na dṛśyate** |
ta**thā hi** kleśa**sammiśraṃ**
dharmadhātur **na dṛśyate** || <3>

ya**thā viśodhi**taṃ kṣīraṃ
ghṛtadravyaṃ **sunirmala**m |
ta**thā viśodhi**tāḥ kleśā
dharmadhātuḥ **sunirmalaḥ** || <4> etc.

2.1.2. Remarks on the text

As usual, there is more correspondence between the words, phrases and sentences of the Skt. and T than the Skt. and Ch. Nevertheless, there are quite a few cases in which one does find a correspondence between the Skt. and Ch that is not evident in T (normally in Ch1, see § 2.3). In some places there are words or phrases in Skt. which have no correspondence in the translations, e.g., *cintayet* <61b> against *bsgrubs pa* <71b> and 可得 {60b}; *āśrayādhimuktānāṃ* <63c> against *theg mchog mos rnams la 'aṅ* [73c] and 勝解

[29] With an error in the 3rd syllable.

[30] With an error in the 4th syllable.

[31] 49c and 59a both with nine syllables.

[32] 64c and 79b have one extra syllable respectively.

行 {62c}; *sarvadharmānāṃ* <78a> against *saṅs rgyas rnams kyi chos kyi* [88a] and 佛法 {77a}; *lakṣaṇa*° <83b> against *ze'u 'bru can* [93b] and 臺 {82b}; *kleśair malinasattvānāṃ* <84c> against *ñon moṅs can gyi sems can gyis* [51c][33] and 煩惱攪擾心 {113c}; °*ajñānadagdhānāṃ* <85c> against *mi śes pas bsgribs pas* [52c] and 少福者 {114c}.[34] In such cases, the Skt. word or phrase is replaced in the edition by a reconstructed form from T or Ch only if the Ms seems incorrect with regard to context or grammar, e.g., *sarvabījeṣu* <16a> for *sarvajīveṣu* in the Ms,[35] or *ajīvaṃ* <59c> for *abīje* in the Ms.[36]

Although within each stanza nearly every word has a parallel in T and Ch, the construction of the sentences in the translations sometimes takes on a new form, with, e.g., shifts in case or number. This can be seen in the following examples:

ya eva dhātuḥ[37] saṃsāre
śodhyamānaḥ sa eva tu |
śuddhaḥ sa eva nirvāṇe
dharmakāyaḥ sa eva hi || <2>[38]

gaṅ źig 'khor ba'i rgyur gyur pa ||
de ñid sbyaṅ ba byas pa las ||
dag pa de ñid mya ṅan 'das ||
chos kyi sku yaṅ de ñid do || [2][39]

---

[33] Strictly speaking.

[34] In the last three examples listed here, the wording of each text is different.

[35] According to the following *pāda*, *sādṛśaṃ jāyate phalam*; T: *de bźin sa bon thams cad las* | *rgyu daṅ 'dra ba'i 'bras bu 'byuṅ*; Ch 1: 如是於諸種 相似生其果.

[36] According to T, *byaṅ chub sems dpa' ma byuṅ bar* [69c].

[37] This word is interpreted differently in T and Ch 1.

[38] "That very element which is in *saṃsāra*, however, is being purified. Purified, it is in *nirvāṇa*, for it is nothing but the Dharmakāya."

[39] "When that which is the cause of *saṃsāra* has been purified, just that, pure, is

其性即生死 淨時亦復然
清淨是涅槃 亦即是法身{2}[40]

and

buddho hi parinirvāti
śucir nityaśubhālayaḥ |
kalpayanti dvayaṃ bālā
advayaṃ yogināṃ padaṃ || <55>[41]

gaṅ phyir saṅs rgyas mya ṅan 'das ||
gtsaṅ ba rtag pa dge ba'i gźi ||
gaṅ phyir gñis ni byis pas brtags ||
de yi gñis med rnal 'byor gnas || [65][42]

是佛般涅槃 常恒淨無垢
愚夫二分別 無二瑜伽句{54}[43]

and

daśabhiś ca balair bālas
tiṣṭhate bālacandravat |
kleśair malinasattvānāṃ

---

nirvāṇa, and nothing but the Dharmakāya." For *dhātu* explained as *hetu*, cf. the passage from the *Ratnagotravibhāgavyākhyā* cited in ZIMMERMANN 2002: 58ff.

40 "Its nature is *saṃsāra*, and when it is purified, it is also like that. When it is pure, it is *nirvāṇa*, and also the Dharmakāya indeed." For *dhātu* explained as "nature", cf. SCHMITHAUSEN 1969: n.116.

41 "For the Buddha enters *pariṇirvāṇa*, pure, with a fundamental basis that is permanent and good. Spiritually immature people conceive duality. For *yogin*s, there is (only) the non-dual abode."

42 "Since the Buddha enters *pariṇirvāṇa*, (he) is pure, and (his) fundamental basis is permanent and good. Since spiritually immature people conceive duality, the *yogin* has his non-dual abode."

43 "This *pariṇirvāṇa* of the Buddha is constantly pure and without stain. (For) spiritually immature people, (it is) the conceiving of duality, (but) the non-dual is the verse of the *yogin*."

na paśyati tathāgatam | <84>[44]

stobs bcu'i stobs kyis byis pa rnams ||
byin brlabs zla ba tshes pa bźin ||
ñon moṅs can gyi sems can gyis ||
de bźin gśegs pa mi mthoṅ ṅo || [51][45]

彼彼人現化[46] 安住如水月
煩惱攪擾心 不見於如來 {113}[47]

etc.

If we make an overview of the entire Skt. text, using T as a basis for its missing conclusion, the contents can be divided into several units. These are, briefly:

1) the relationship between gnosis (*jñāna*) and defilement (*kleśa*), <1-23>
2) emptiness, <24-37>
3) the true nature of the six senses and their objects, <38-45>
4) the need to relinquish the conception of
   a. self and <46-50>
   b. objects, <51-55>[61-65]
5) the path <56-63>[66-73]
6) a. introduction of the *bhūmi*s of the bodhisattva, <64-67>[74-77]
   b. the ten *bhūmi*s of the bodhisattva, <68-77>[78-

---

[44] "On account of the ten powers the spiritually immature man stands like the new moon. Because of the defilements of impure beings he does not see the *tathāgata*."

[45] "Spiritually immature people are empowered by the ten powers, like the new moon. The being with defilements does not see the *tathāgata*."

[46] This *pāda* has no correspondence in the other texts. However it is clear that the object of this sentence, which is equivalent to the subject in Skt. and T, is plural as in T, against the singular in Skt.

[47] "One after the other, (he) appears before their eyes and tranquilly abides, like the moon reflecting on the water. (Since) defilements disturb the heart, (they) don't see the *tathāgata*."

87]

7) the Dharmakāya, <78-80>[88-90]
8) the Nirmāṇakāya for
   a. the bodhisattvas who have arrived at the *bhūmi*s (Buddhaputras), <81-83>[91-93]
   b. the normal living beings, and the Rūpakāya, <84-86c, *86d-88>[51-55]
9) the Sambhogakāya, <*89-93>[56-60]
10) the Buddha. <*94-101>[94-101]

This breakdown reveals the logical, thematic structure of the DDhS and its organic development (some verses, however, may be insertions). The author commences by introducing the Dharmadhātu and elucidating how it is obscured by the defilements (*kleśa*s); he then proceeds to explain selflessness (*anātman*) – of the Self, sense-objects, indeed of all things – demonstrating that conceptuality prevents and is not involved in awakening (*bodhi*). Subsequent to this, he expounds the components of the path to liberation, presents the *bhūmi*s and finally describes Buddhahood and the Buddha.

It is interesting to note that in all versions, the contents of the first half of the hymn, stanzas 1-50, apart from some omissions, form a fixed and integral text.[48] However, from stanza 51 on the order of the stanzas differ in Skt. and T, despite there being a word-for-word correspondence in the individual stanzas' translations. Here, the order found in Ch1 and Ch2 is closer to the Skt., if one disregards some omissions. Stanzas <51-83> of the Skt. correspond to stanzas [61-93] of T. Stanzas <50-51> in the critical edition read as follows:

uktaṃ ca sūtravargeṣu
viharaty ātmacintakaḥ |

[48] However, Atiśa's *Dharmadhātudarśanagīti* quotes ca. 20 stanzas from the first 32 stanzas of the DDhS in a different order, which is difficult to explain. Cf. SEYFORT RUEGG 1971: 471 and n. 119.

prajñādīpavihāreṇa
paramāṃ śāntim āgataḥ || <50>

na bodher dūraṃ sañjñī syān |
na sāsannaṃ ca sañjñinaḥ |
ṣaṇṇāṃ hi viṣayābhāso |
yathābhūtaṃ parijñayā || <51>[49]

These correspond to T [50 and 61], Ch1 {49-50}, Ch2 (49-50):

śes rab mar me la gnas nas ||
mchog tu źi bar gyur pa yis ||
bdag la brtags pas gnas bya źes ||
mdo sde 'i tshogs las gsuṅs pa lags || [50]

byaṅ chub riṅ bar mi bsam źiṅ ||
ñe bar yaṅ ni bsam mi bya ||
yul drug snaṅ ba med par ni ||
yaṅ dag ji bźin rig gyur pa'o || [61]

說於眾契經 住於自思惟
照以智慧燈 即得最勝寂 {49}

菩提不遠想 亦無隣近想
是六境影像 皆由如是知 {50}

煩惱籠迷執 世尊經所宣
智生惑染滅 妄執勿相纏 (49)

---

[49] "And, it has been said in the group of Sūtras: 'He remains reflecting on himself. Through abiding in the lamp of wisdom, he has reached the supreme peace.' One who is aware would not be far from (the state of) awakening; nor would that (awakening) be in the proximity of the one who is aware. For with the knowledge that is in accord with reality there is (only) a false appearance of the objects of the six (sense faculties)."

去來執最勝 體空猶可思
菩提非妄執 正證亦知非 (50)

From Skt. stanza <84>, once again the stanza order is no longer the same in the four texts under consideration. Stanzas <83-84> read as follows:

anekaratnapattrābhaṃ
lakṣaṇojjvalakalpikaṃ |
anekaiḥ padmakoṭībhiḥ
samantāt parivāritam || <83>[50]

daśabhiś ca balair bālas
tiṣṭhate bālacandravat |
kleśair malinasattvānāṃ
na paśyati tathāgatam || <84>

These correspond to T [93, 51], Ch1 {82, 113} and Ch2 (75, 83).

'dab ma rin chen du ma'i 'od ||
'dod par bya ba'i ze'u 'bru can ||
pad ma bye ba du ma yis ||
rnam pa kun tu yoṅs su bskor || [93]

stobs bcu'i stobs kyis byis pa rnams ||
byin brlabs zla ba tshes pa bźin ||
ñon moṅs can gyi sems can gyis ||
de bźin gśegs pa mi mthoṅ ṅo || [51]

無量寶葉光 寶光明為臺
無量億蓮花 普遍為眷屬 {82}

---

[50] "(The seat) is characterized by the light of its many jewel petals, which is like fire. It is surrounded by many millions of lotuses on all sides."

彼彼人現化 安住如水月
煩惱攪擾心 不見於如來 {113}

大寶花王座 俱胝眾妙成
莊嚴皆普遍 功德實難思 (75)

況似頗胝寶 隨緣現影同
物情根有感 周普事無窮 (80)[51]

On the basis of this comparison of the stanzas, it might be possible to conclude that these units, if in fact they were even recognized as units, were freely selected and combined with one another at the will of the compilers. Since the order and number of stanzas in the various texts is not identical, the meaning of the text varies correspondingly in the different versions.

Indisputably, since there are many variations between the Sanskrit and the DDhS translations due to their different transmission backgrounds,[52] a comparison of sentences and contexts would be less fruitful than one confined to words and short phrases. Thus the critical apparatus operates solely with deviations from the Skt. of words and short phrases, viz., small units of words.

2.2. Tibetan translation

The following Tibetan translations of the DDhS have been used in the critical edition. The location in each canonical version is as follows:

---

[51] It is doubtful whether this stanza really corresponds to stanza 84 in the Skt. text, cf. TSUKINOWA 1933: 532 and HAYASHIMA 1987: 64.

[52] For examples of various Skt. Mss. and T, cf. MACDONALD 2005: xxxiii-xxxvi and STEINKELLNER 2007: xxxvii-xliv.

Co ne (C): ka, fols. 72a7-76b4
sDe dge (D): ka, fols. 63b5-67b3
dGa' ldan (Golden Ms Edition, G): ka, fols. 90b1-96a1
sNar thang (N): ka, fols. 70a3-74b3
Peking (Qianlong, P): ka, fols. 73a7-77a8

As mentioned above, Skt. and T correspond more than Skt. and Ch, although this is not consistently the case. There are also instances where the Skt. only corresponds to the Ch (see § 3.2), T corresponds only to Ch (see § 2.1.2), or T does not correspond to any other text (see § 2.1.2).

Seyfort Ruegg (1971: notes on pp. 464-471) points out many variant readings in D against the other editions.[53] When compared with the Skt. text, these distinctive readings in D often seem more reliable, i.e., are closer to the Skt., than the reading shared by the remaining four editions, e.g.: *saṅs rgyas ñid* D instead of *sñiṅ po ñid* CGNP [15c] for *buddhatvam* <15c>[54]; *brtags pa* D instead of *btags pa* CGNP [30b] for *kalpyamānaṃ* <30b>; *brtags pa* D instead of *btags pa* CGNP [30d] for *kalpitaṃ* <30d>[55]; *chos kyi dbyiṅs kyi ṅo bo yin* D instead of *chos kyi dbyiṅs kyi ṅo bo yis* CGNP[56] [41c] for *dharmadhātusvabhāvatā* <41d>; *mthoṅ* D instead of *mtho* CGNP [46a] for *dṛṣṭaṃ* <46a>[57]; *bdag la brtags pas gnas bya źes* D instead of *bdag la rtag par gnas bya źes* CGNP[58] [50c] for *viharaty ātmacintakaḥ* <50b>; *brtags* D instead of *btags* GNP and *gtags* C [65c] for *kalpayanti* <55c>[59]; and so on. But not all of the readings in D are correct, e.g.: *dri ma* CGNP instead of *ñon moṅs* D [21c] for *malaṃ* <21c>; *zab pa la* CGNP instead of *zad pa la* D [83c]

[53] Neither the Skt. Ms nor G was available to him.

[54] Ch1 佛體 = **buddhakāya* {15c}.

[55] Ch1 分別 {29bd}.

[56] Ch1 法界自性故 = **dharmadhātusvabhāvatvāt* {40d}.

[57] Ch1 見 {45a}.

[58] Ch1 住於自思惟 {49b}.

[59] Ch1 分別 {54c}.

for °*gambhīrā* <73c>[60]; *mi g.yo ba* CGNP instead of *mi g.yos pa* D [85d] for *akampyā* <75d>; and so on.

As compared to the Skt. text, the second *pāda* of stanza [33] is missing in T. In CGNP, a *pāda* has been added between stanzas [91] and [92], perhaps in order to bring the total number of *pāda*s into balance. This added *pāda* is merely a repetition of the third *pāda* of [92]. In D, this odd *pāda* is absent, although it also lacks the *pāda* of [33].[61]

More noteworthy is the shift of a block of ten stanzas in T. As has been described above, stanzas <51-83> of the Skt. text correspond to [61-93] of T, although from the beginning to stanza [50], T parallels the Skt. text stanza for stanza. Stanzas [51-60] correspond to <84-86c> (and presumably the following stanzas) of the Skt.[62]

To explain this variation, there are three hypotheses:

1. The Tibetan translators revised the text during translation, finding their order more suitable with regard to the context than the original one. Stanzas [51-60] (which would correspond to <84-*93> in the Skt. text) are related to three *kāya*s of the Buddha. The first *kāya*, namely Dharmakāya, the Nirmāṇakāya for the Bodhisattvas, and the Buddha, which are involved with Buddhahood, are then consecutively described in [88-93] and [94-101], without the interruption as found in the Skt. While the insertion of the topic of the three *kāya*s of the Buddha between 3) "the true nature of the six senses and their objects" and 4) "the need to relinquish the conception" is not particularly reasonable, it seems logical to want to connect the two parts concerning the Dharmakāya etc.

2. The translators jumped when reading their Skt. exemplar, overlooking ten stanzas, namely <84-*93>. Like the

---

60 Ch1 甚深 {72c}.

61 This has been noted in SEYFORT RUEGG (1971: 471 and n. 117) and HAYASHIMA (1987: 44); Seyfort Ruegg, however, considers the proper position of the additional *pāda* to be stanza [99].

62 Due to the missing final folio of the Skt. text, it is not certain whether the Skt. would have corresponded to all ten stanzas of T.

first *pāda* in <84>, *daśabhiś ca balair bālas*,[63] the Sanskrit for the first *pāda* in [94], *stobs bcu po yis yoṅs su gaṅ*, quite possibly also began with *daśabhiḥ* and was followed closely by *balaiḥ*, which may have led to the eye-skip. When discovered, the forgotten stanzas were inserted into the text at an earlier point, namely following stanza [50].

3. The Skt. exemplar used by the Tibetan translators presented the verse order as now found in T. However, since both Chinese translations confirm the stanza order of our Skt. text, their Skt. text may have had an error, i.e., the Tibetan translators had a Skt. Ms that already had the verses either inserted in the wrong place or written around the margins or on an extra folio. This would mean that a Skt. scribe committed the eye-skip, as described in the second hypothesis, and that the translators had to deal with his ten added stanzas.

Although there has still been no convincible evidence for the using of a Sanskrit manuscript during the redaction of D, it is nevertheless clear that after the redaction D seems closer to Skt. than the other editions among most alternative readings. Therefore we use D as the basic text for the critical edition of the Tibetan translation.[64] However, if a reading in the other version(s) has been found to be closer to the Skt. than that in D, and thus is more reliable, this is then the reading that has been chosen.[65] In stanzas [56-60] as well as the preface and colophon, for which there is no Skt. or Ch parallel text available, the T edition follows D if there is no clear contradiction with regard to context or grammar; otherwise the common mode of textual criticism is followed, e.g., *'phags pa 'jam dpal gźon nur gyur pa* D instead of *'jam dpal gźon nur gyur pa* CGNP in the preface, but *'phags pa klu sgrub* CGNP instead of *chen po klu sgrub* D in the colophon. In the critical apparatus of T, variations in punctuation or ab-

---

[63] *stobs bcu'i stobs kyis byis pa rnams* (T).

[64] As shown above, it can be seen that D is often the closest to the Skt. original.

[65] Where no Skt. correspondence is found, a comparison with Ch has been made, e.g. *des* CGNP instead of *te* D [96c] for 以 {85a}.

breviated forms, like *ñido*, *yoṅsu*, etc., which mostly occur in G and N, have not been taken into account.

2.3. Chinese translations

The earlier Chinese translation (Ch1) is found in Taishō 413, and the later (Ch2) in Taishō 1675.[66] The title of Ch1 reads 百千頌大集經地藏菩薩請問法身讚 (**Kṣitigarbhaparipṛcchādharmakāyastava*), "Hymn concerning Kṣitigarbha guestion on the Dharmakāya in the *Mahāsannipāta* which consists of [proses whose amount equals] hundred-thousand Ślokas". Here, neither a relationship with the topic of the Dharmadhātu, nor the author Nāgārjuna is indicated. In the eighth century, this text was regarded as an appendix to the *Mahāsannipātasūtra* and was attributed to Kṣitigarbha.

Ch1 is a direct translation of the DDhS and in its entirety contains 125 four-*pāda* stanzas. While in the first 124 stanzas each *pāda* has five syllables, which is normally regarded as an apt reflection of the Skt. metre *anuṣṭubh*,[67] each *pāda* in the final stanza has seven syllables, which might correspond to the Skt. metre *triṣṭubh*. Verses {1-82} match stanzas <1-83> of the Skt. text very well, except that stanza <20> in the latter finds no equivalent in Ch1. Naturally there are here, too, a handful of variations in the wording.[68] It seems that stanzas {83-90} of Ch1 would be equivalent to

---

[66] Ch2 has long been recognized as a Chinese translation of the DDhS; see, e.g., Seyfort Ruegg 1971: 463. In 1933, Tsukinowa discovered that Ch1 was an earlier Chinese translation, but not all scholars took note; it has been mentioned in Hayashima (1987) and Brunnhölzl (2007: 113). Like Tsukinowa (1933), Hayashima (1987) also provides a detailed comparison of T, Ch1 and Ch2; however, Hayashima does not take advantage of this comparison or of the critical apparatus in the Taishō edition to improve certain readings in the main text of Ch1.

[67] For the term 五言四句, see Taishō 2059, 415b and Mair & Mei 1991: 454.

[68] Cf. notes 83-85.

*94-101 of the Skt. text. Surprisingly, some of the same portion of the text that does not correspond in position to the Skt. and T (i.e., [51-60]) is again not in the expected position in Ch1. However, contrary to T, these stanzas (in this case five: {113-115 and 120, 122}) have been placed at the end, i.e., {113-115} correspond to <51-53>; {120} corresponds to T [54], and {122} to T [55]. Stanzas {91-121, 123-124}[69] deal with the Nirmāṇakāya, which also here can be divided into two parts. The first twelve stanzas {91-112} describe the Nirmāṇakāya from the side of the Buddhas; the latter eleven {113-121, 123-124} describe the Nirmāṇakāya in the eyes of ordinary beings. In addition, 22 stanzas, {91-112}, reveal Tantric characteristics and find no parallel among other three texts.[70] The last stanza {125} describes the spreading of this doctrine.

Ch2 bears the title 贊法界頌 (**Dharmadhātustava* or *Dharmadhātustotra*). It is a less satisfactory translation,[71] and contains only 87 four-*pāda* stanzas. It is clear that many stanzas of the Skt. text are missing, while at least nine stanzas[72] find no correspondence in any other version and the correspondence of more than ten stanzas is unclear. In any case, stanzas (1-75) can be recognized as a translation of stanzas <1-83> of the Skt. text, in the same order. Thus, Ch2 corresponds until verse (75) to both Ch1 and the Skt. text. The next four stanzas, (76-79), may have corresponded to *94-101 of the Skt. text. Then follow stanzas (80-86) on the Nirmāṇakāya and Sambhogakāya, which correspond to stanzas <84-86c> and possibly *86d-92 of the Skt. text. The concluding stanza deals with the spreading of the work.

There is some vocabulary in the Skt. text that corre-

---

69 Stanza {122} deals with the Rūpakāya, cf. the breakdown in §2.1.2.

70 Cf. TSUKINOWA 1933: 540ff. Tsukinowa believed, therefore, that this part must have been added even after the establishment of the common content of DDhS, and that Ch1's entire text would stand after that of T and Ch2 in the transmission line, cf. ibid., 425ff.

71 On the quality of translations during the Song Dynasty, see SEN 2002: 27-80.

72 Stanzas (3, 14, 28, 61, 74, 83, 84, 86, 87).

sponds only to words found in Ch, e.g., 石藏 {9c} for *pāṣāṇakośe* <9c> against *rdo yi naṅ na* [9c]; 煩惱海 {15b} for *kleśasāgare* <15b> against *ñon moṅs gzeb* [15b]; 二形 (24b) for °*napuṃsakam* <24b> against *skyes pa* [24b] and 男 {23b}; 無色亦無形 {39b} for *arūpam anidarśanaṃ* <40b> against *gzugs su med pa'i dpe* [40b]; 器 {52b} for *bhājane* <53b> against *lus 'dir* [63b]; 稻芽 {62a}[73] for *śālyāṅkurādīnāṃ* <63a> against *sā lu'i sa bon sogs* [73a]; 得生 {65d} for *jāyate* <66d> against *rdzogs śiṅ gsal* [76d][74]; 常當於佛法 {66b} for *buddhe dharme ca nityaśaḥ* <67b> against *saṅs rgyas chos daṅ dge 'dun la* | *rtag tu mos pa brtan po yis* | [77ab]; 覺悟 {67c} for *avabhodhena* <68c> against *ṅes rtogs pa* [78c]; 照耀得離垢 {69b} for *prabhābhrājav-inirmalā* <70b> against *dri med śes rab rab gsal bas* [80b]; 生死海 {82b} for *bhavasāgarāt* <82b> against *'khor ba'i gzeb las* [92b]; and 有情 {115a} for *sattvānām* <86a> against *dman pa* [53a]. There are also some words that Ch1 shares with T but not with the Skt. (see § 2.1.2).

In addition to these two Chinese translations, there exists another translation, whose authority is however doubtful.[75] It is the second 品 (*parivarta*) called 地藏菩薩讃歎法身觀行品 (**Kṣitigarbhadharmakāyastavasaṃskāra-parīkṣāparivarta*), "The Chapter of Investigation on Predispositions, in which Kṣitigarbha Bodhisattva praises the Dharmakāya", in a Sūtra called 示所犯者瑜伽法鏡經, "Sūtra of the Yogadharma Mirror, revealing those who offended (the Discipline)", in Taishō 2896. Recorded in a Buddhist canon register from A.D. 730, it has already been acknowledged as an Apocrypha,[76] and was therefore proba-

[73] It is possible that the phrase 守護稻穀種 芽莖必得生 (57ab) also corresponds to {62a}.

[74] Probably 顯法身 法身理無缺 (60cd) supports T.

[75] It is identified by TSUKINOWA (1934: 46ff.).

[76] In 開元釋教錄, "Register of the Buddhist [Canon] in the Kaiyuan Era", cf.

bly regarded as lost. This Sūtra is only preserved in the form of a fragment found in Dunhuang,[77] in which its first *parivarta* and most of the second *parivarta* is no longer available. According to its colophon, this Sūtra was translated into Chinese by 室利末多 (*Śrīmadda) in A.D. 707. If we can rely on this dating, then it seems possible that this *parivarta* may be neither an invention nor a re-composition based on Ch1, a Chinese translation which was finished more than 50 years later than this text, but indeed the earliest translation of the DDhS.[78]

This second *parivarta* (henceforth: ChX) contains only 31 four-*pāda* stanzas, in which each *pāda* has seven syllables, and a final paragraph in prose, but no indication regarding the original total number of stanzas[79] has come down to us. Most of these stanzas correspond approximately to {90-125} of Ch1 in wording and order, while stanzas x+22-24 correspond to <84-86> in Skt. and [51-53] in T, and x+1 and x+29 to [101] and [54] in T too. Nevertheless eight stanzas, {98-102} and {122-124}, have no correspondence in ChX, whereas three stanzas, x+2, 8, 14, do not find a match in any other texts.[80] When we compare the stanzas with those of other texts, especially x+22-24 with {113-115} and <84-86> as follows, we can see that ChX is a more paraphrastic and literary translation than Ch1.[81]

隨諸眾生示神變　　猶如明月水中現

Taishō 2154, 627b29-c12. However, it is not definitively stated there that the second *parivarta* itself is either a rewriting of an old Sūtra or an apocryphal one at all, cf. TSUKINOWA 1934: 49.

77 For its preservation, cf. YABUKI 1927: 232.

78 Its content also appears to support this assumption, cf. below.

79 For the numbering of these stanzas "x+1", "x+2" and so forth are used by the text edition in ChX.

80 To explain these variations further research is required.

81 Seven Chinese syllables for one *pāda* seems to be too many if we assume that the hymn part in the Skt. exemplar of ChX was also written in *anuṣṭubh* metre; cf. n. 67.

邪智生盲惡眾生　佛對面前而不現 x+22

譬如餓鬼臨大海　盡見海水皆枯竭
如是薄德惡眾生　口常說言無有佛 x+23

此等薄德有情類　諸佛如來不能救
譬如生盲無目人　明珠對前而不見 x+24[82]

彼彼人現化 安住如水月
煩惱攪擾心 不見於如來 {113}

如餓鬼於海 普遍見枯竭
如是少福者 無佛作分別 {114}

有情少福者 如來云何作
如於生盲手 安以最勝寶 {115}[83]

daśabhiś ca balair bālas
tiṣṭhate bālacandravat |
kleśair malinasattvānāṃ
na paśyati tathāgatam || <84>

yadā pretāḥ samantāt tu

---

[82] "He demonstrates his supernatural power according to (the merit of) each being (respectively), like the moon reflected on the water (surface). For those evil beings who have deviant intelligence and are born blind, the Buddha does stand before them, yet does not show himself. Like the ghosts in front of ocean only see that it becomes dry everywhere, such evil beings, whose merit is inferior, often say 'the Buddha doesn't exist'. All the *tathāgata* Buddhas can not rescue such sentient beings, whose virtue is meager, like a man who is born blind without eyes and cannot see the bright pearl in front of him."

[83] "Like the ghosts on the shore, who see that it becomes dry everywhere, such ones, whose merit is inferior, have the idea 'the Buddha doesn't exist'. For the sentient beings, whose merit is inferior, what will the *tathāgata* do? In the same way one puts the supreme of jewels in the hand of a man who is born blind."

śuṣkaṃ paśyanti sāgaram |
tathaivājñānadagdhānāṃ
buddho nāstīti kalpanā || <85>

sattvānām alpapuṇyānāṃ
bhagavān kiṃ kariṣyati |
jātya xx ◡--x
xxxx ◡-◡x || <86>[84]

We are therefore convinced that ChX represents an independent translation from a Skt. manuscript in the DDhS transmission lineage. Finally, according to ChX's prose part, the whole hymn is placed in the mouth of Kṣitigarbha, whose name appears in the title of ChX and Ch1. Hence it is obvious that before the middle of the eighth century it was not thought that Nāgārjuna authored the text.

Thus, Ch1 serves as the main Chinese text for our detailed comparison; Ch2 and ChX are only mentioned where necessary. These other two texts are used primarily only for the sake of textual comparison, and thus the Taishō edition is sufficient for our purposes. A so-called critical edition will be made for Ch1, in which a reading from either the main Taishō text or its critical apparatus (CAT) will be chosen based on its Skt. and/or T parallel, if it has one. When stanzas have no parallel, or their parallel provides little help, the reading will be determined based on context (e.g. 覺悟 for 令舉 in {108c}) or grammar (e.g. 渡 for 度 in {81b}; 猶如 for 由如 in {99a}). As the Ch2 translation dates to the later period of Buddhism's spread in China, its transmission period has been comparatively short and thus only a few variations have been handed down. The main Taishō text is thus used for Ch2, without any revised readings. Nevertheless, apart from a few vocabulary correspondences such as 明了

84 "The pretas see the ocean but it becomes dry everywhere; in just the same way do those who are burned by ignorance have the false conception that 'the Buddha does not exist'. What will/can the Blessed One do for beings with little merit? It is as if one puts the best of jewels in the hand of a man who is born blind." The translation for *pāda* c and d in <86> is based on T.

(6d) for *bhāsate* <5d> and 照燿 {5d} against *mthoṅ* [5d], etc., the content of Ch2 stands too far from the other texts to be of much special use. Since YABUKI (1927: 233-236) made a critical edition of ChX, which has been taken over into Taishō, and since the Skt. and T parallels do not help to improve the critical apparatus, ChX here follows the text in Taishō.

3. Conclusion

Thus, we see that through the long textual transmission of the *Dharmadhātustava*, the main textual constituent has been stanzas 1-83, with the insertion of the Nirmāṇa- and Sambhogakāya descriptions of T [51-60] an anomaly. The presumed positioning of these, <84-86c> and *86d-93, in the Skt. text, between the two parts of the Dharmakāya description, is a special case too, since in the other three versions, [94-101], {83-90}, (76-79), the description of the Dharmakāya is found as an integral section.

The core of this text already existed in the eighth century, albeit with another title. It spread widely, as the Sūtra was affiliated with Tantrism together with texts traditionally associated with Nāgārjuna. Only after the end of the eighth century, or even as late as the eleventh century, was the hymn ascribed to Nāgārjuna and given the title *Dharmadhātustava*. At this time it appears to have been shortened. Revisions occurred during its translation and transmission in the respective importing lands. The order in Ch2 is 1-8a, 10 and 8b-9, viz., the most ideal transmission in spite of its translation. The order in the second part of the Skt. text is not reasonable and has no echo in other versions. The order in T is 1-4a, 8b-9, 4b-8a and 10. It might have been the same as in Ch2 if the translators/redactors had not misread the text.

Conventions and Abbreviations

• Conventions in the text[1]

a. Folio numbers are indicated in the margin and with subscript.
b. The stanza numbering of the Skt. text is placed in angled brackets < >, that of T in square brackets [ ], of Ch1 in braces {} and of Ch2 in round brackets ( ).
c. Missing *pāda*s are replaced by corresponding marks for metre, e.g., in Skt. xxxx ⏑--x for odd *pāda*s and xxxx ⏑-⏑x for even *pāda*s; xxxxxxx for *pāda*s in T.
d. Punctuation in the form of *daṇḍa*s and double *daṇḍa*s, as well as division into paragraphs is editorial.
e. *avagraha*s are editorial.
f. Orthography and *sandhi*:
   a) *ba* and *va*, being indistinguishable from each other, have been read according to expectation.
   b) Irregular use of the sibilants *śa*, *ṣa*, *sa*, and of *kṣ*, *k*, viz. of *kṣy* and *ky*, and the reverse have been read according to expectation without being reported.
   c) Redundant and mostly undeleted *anusvāra*, usually before m in the form *ṃm*, are not reported.
   d) The following orthographical variants are not reported:
      • gemination of consonants after a semi-vowel (most frequently after *-r*)

---

[1] Including signs in the introduction.

- degemination of consonants before a semi-vowel (most frequently before *v*-)
- use of *anusvāra* for homorganic nasal or the reverse
- use of class sibilant for *visarga* before a sibilant
- non-application of *sandhi*
- non-occurrence of *avagraha*

e) *sandhi*: the classical rules of *sandhi* have been consistently applied.[2]

• Conventions of the critical apparatus

Reference is to the lines of the page above and the location indicated by the superscript asterisk. References to the same line are separated by a small centered circle.

As a rule, deletions, corrections and additions *in margine* in the manuscript are only reported if the resulting reading is not accepted. Also not reported are missing *virāma*s. When helpful for explaining different readings and *sandhi*, *daṇḍa*s are reported. All variants are given with all peculiarities of the manuscript's reading in regard to orthography, deletions and, occasionally, punctuation.

[2] Cf. Louis Renou, *Grammaire sanscrite*. Paris 1996, §43. Following Renou, in the case of external *sandhi* we prefer the media before initial nasals, but following general scholarly usage, full assimilation of final *t* and *d*.

• Editorial signs in the apparatus:[3]

.	illegible part of an *akṣara* due, e.g., to being out of focus
..	illegible *akṣara* due, e.g., to being out of focus
‹ ›	contain *akṣara*(s) added later by the scribe or by another hand
'	*avagraha*
|	*daṇḍa*
||	double *daṇḍa*
o	a circle between two *daṇḍa*s or two double *daṇḍa*s, serving as a punctuation marker
×	empty space in the manuscript equivalent to the size of approximately one *akṣara*
^	sign of insertion added above the line
ˇ	sign of insertion added below the line
< >	contain emendational additions (with no space in the manuscript)
{ }	contain *akṣara*(s) deleted in the manuscript by means of one or two small strokes
{{}}	contain *akṣara*(s) deleted in the manuscript by means of erasure
ʘ	string-hole
( )	contain *akṣara*(s) or part(s) of an *akṣara* unclear due, e.g., to being out of focus in the photocopy
*	*virāma*
?	uncertain
	signs for *siddham*

[3] Including signs in the introduction.

Abbreviations:

AAS	Austrian Academy of Sciences
ac	*ante correctionem*
add.	added in
BHSD	*Buddhist Hybrid Sanskrit Grammar and Dictionary, vol. II: Dictionary*, ed. Franklin Edgerton. New Haven: Yale University Press 1953.
BHSG	*Buddhist Hybrid Sanskrit Grammar and Dictionary, vol. I: Grammar*, ed. Franklin Edgerton. New Haven: Yale University Press 1953.
C	Co ne bsTan 'gyur: Electronic Edition from Tibetan Buddhist Resource Center (TBRC)
CAT	critical apparatus in Taishō
cf.	confer
Ch	Chinese or Chinese text
Ch1	百千頌大集經地藏菩薩請問法身讚, Taishō 413
Ch2	讚法界頌, Taishō 1675
ChX	地藏菩薩讚歎法身觀行品 in 示所犯者瑜伽法鏡經, Taishō 2896
conj.	conjectured
CPD	*A Critical Pāli Dictionary*, begun by V. Trenckner, eds. Dines Andersen et al. Copenhagen: The Royal Danish Academy 1924-.
CTRC	China Tibetology Research Center
D	sDe dge bsTan 'gyur: Electronic edition from the TBRC
DDhS	*Dharmadhātustava*
em.	emendated

EWAia	*Etymologisches Wörterbuch des Altindoarischen*, ed. MANFRED MAYRHOFER, Heidelberg: Carl Winter Universitätsverlag 1986-2001.
G	dGa' ldan bsTan 'gyur, Golden Mss Edition: Electronic edition from the TBRC
m.c.	*metri causa*
Ms(s)	manuscript(s)
N	sNar thang bsTan 'gyur: Electronic edition from the TBRC
om.	omitted in
P	(Qianlong) Peking bsTan 'gyur: *The Tibetan Tripiṭaka. Peking Edition*, Otani University, Kyoto, ed. by SUZUKI DAISETZ T., Kyoto 1955-61.
^{pc}	*post correctionem*
Skt.	Sanskrit or Sanskrit text
STTAR	Sanskrit Texts from the Tibetan Autonomous Region
SUṬ	*Sekoddeśaṭīkā* of Nāropā
T	Tibetan or Tibetan text
TBRC	Tibetan Buddhist Resource Center Library *<www.tbrc.org>*
Taishō	*Taishō Shinshū Daizōkyō*, 100 vols., Tokyo, 1924-.
TAR	Tibetan Autonomous Region

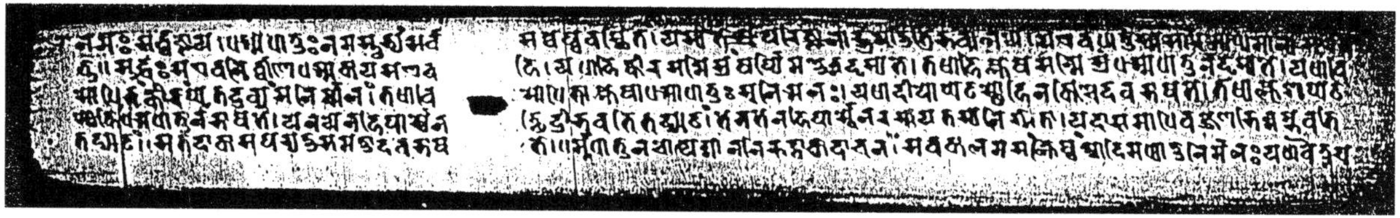

Folio 1a of *Dharmadhātustava*

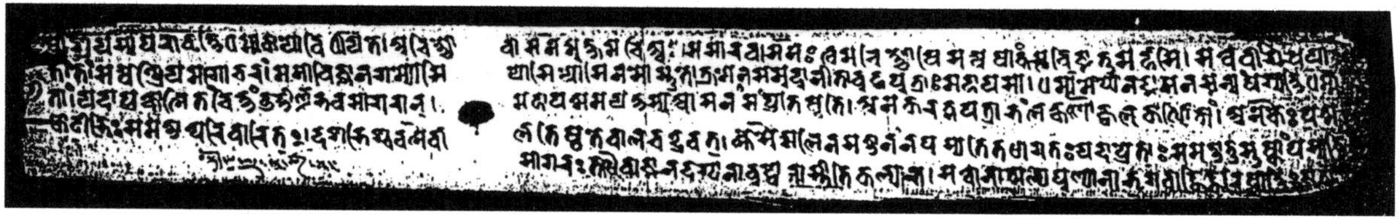

Folio 5b of *Dharmadhātustava*

Diplomatic Edition

1a

1a1 ? namaḥ sarvvajñāya | dharmmadhātuḥ namas tubhyaṃ sarvaʘsatveṣv avasthita | yasya te aparijñānād bhramanti tribhavālaye | ya eva dhātus sa(ṃ)sāre sodhyamānya (sa eva)
1a2 tu || suddhaḥ sa eva nirvvāṇe dharmmakāya sa eva ʘ hi | yathā hi kṣīrasamisraṃ ṣarppimaṇḍan na dṛsyate | tathā hi kleṣasanmisraṃ dharmmadhātur na dṛsyate | yathā vi
1a3 sodhitaṃ kṣīraṃ ghṛtadravyaṃ sanirmmalaṃ | tathā viʘsodhitā kleṣā dharmādhātuḥ sunirmalaḥ || yathā dīpo ghaṭastho hi na kiñcid avabhāṣate | tathā kleśaghaṭa
1a4 stho hi dharmadhātur na bhāṣate | yena yena hi pārsvena ʘ cchidrībhavati tad ghaṭaṃ | tena tena hi pārsvena rasmaya tasya nirggatā | yadā samādhivajreṇa bhinnam bhavati
1a5 tad ghaṭaṃ || sa tadākāsaparyanta samantād avabhāṣaʘte | dharmmadhātu na cotpannā na niruddhā kadācana^{v}‹ṃ› || sarvakālam asaṃkliṣṭhaṃ ādimadhyāntanirmalaḥ | yathā vaiḍūrya

1b

1b1 ratnaṃ hi sarvakālap(r)abhās(v)aram* | pāṣāṇako(ṣe) saṃcchaʘnna ābhā ta(sya) na r(ā)jate | evaṃ hi kleṣasaṃc-channo dha(r)madhātuḥ sanirmalaḥ nāso bhrājati sam*sāre ni(r)vāṇ(e)
1b2 tat prabhāsvaraḥ | gotre (vā satti$^{?}$) vyāyāma jātarūpan(i)ʘdarssanāt* || gotre asati vyāyāma sramaḥ kev-alam (i)ṣyate || ahaṃ yathā hi tuṣagacchantaṃ na dhānyaṃ tat phalaṃ mataḥ
1b3 tathā hi kleṣasaṃcchannā nāsau (byaddhe)ti kalpyate | yaʘ(thā) hi tu(ṣa)nirmuktaṃ tat phalaṃ pratibhāṣate | tathā hi kleṣanirmukto dharmakāya ṣrabhāvyate | upa kriyate loke
1b4 kadal(y)ā nāsti sārata | phalāni tasya sārāṇi bhaʘkyate amṛtopamāḥ | evaṃ hy asāre sāsāre nirvṛte kleṣasāgare || phalan tasyāpi buddhatvaṃm amṛtaṃ sarvade
1b5 hināṃ | evaṃ hi sarvajīveṣu sādṛsyaṃ jāyate phalaṃ | ʘ jīvair vinā phalaṃ nāsti ka prājñaḥ pratipats(y)ete | bījabhūtas tasau dhātuḥ dharmānām āsrayo mataḥ | sodhyamā

2a

2a1 na krameṇaivaṃ buddhatvaspadam āvahet* | nirmālau (candra)Θsūryau hi āvṛtau pañcabhir malaiḥ | abhranīhāra-dhūmena rāhuvaktrarajādibhiḥ evaṃ prabhāsvaraṃ cittam ā
2a2 vṛtt̨aṃ pañcabhir malaiḥ | kāmavyāpādamithyena audhatyaṃΘvicikiṃtsayā | agnisaucaṃ yathā vastraṃ malina vividhair malaiḥ agnimadhye yathā kṣiptaṃ malaṃ dagdhaṃ na va
2a3 stratā | evaṃ prabhāsvaraṃ cittaṃ malinaṃ rāgajair mal(aiḥ) Θ jñānāgninā malaṃ dagdhaṃ na ddhagdhaṃ tat prabhāsvaraṃ | sūnyatāhārakā subhrāḥ ye kecid bhāṣitā jinaiḥ | sarvās tāḥ
ow 4+4 **2a4** kleśavyāvṛttī naiva dhātor vināsanam* | pṛthivyāntaΘr-hitān toyaṃ yathā tiṣthati nirrmalam* | kleśair antaritaṃ jñānaṃ tathā ‸‹bhā›ti ‸‹su›nirmalaṃ | dharmmadhāpu yadā nātmā na
2a5 ca strīnanapunsakaṃ | sarvagrāhavini(r)muktaṃ katham āΘmm(e)ti kalpyate ||

2b

2b1 savva dharmā hy asaṃsaktāḥ strī(ṣuṃ)stvaṃ hi na vidyate | rāgāΘ(tva)vinayā(r)thāya strīpustvaṃ pradarśitaṃ | anityaduḥkhaṃ sūnyeti cittanidhyaptayaḥs trayaḥ paramā cittani
2b2 dhyapti dharmāṇā nisvabhāvatā | yathā hi garbho garbhiṇyāṃ Θ vidyate na ca dṛsyate | tathā hi kleśasaṃc-channaṃ dharma(tā)tvaṃ na dṛśyate | caturṇṇāṃ hi vikalpāṇāṃ utpattir bhūtabhau
2b3 tikā | ahaṃmamavikalpo ti nāmasaṃjñānimitt(ā)jaṃ Θ praṇidhānaṃ hi buddhāṇāṃ nirābhāṣam alakṣaṇām* | pratyātmayogitvād buddhāṇā(ṃ) nityadharmatā | yathā śaśaviṣā
2b4 ṇā hi kalpyamāna na vidyate | tathā hi sarvva-dharmmeΘṣu kalpitaṃ naiva vidyate | paramānurajaḥ kintu govidvānaṃ na vidyate | yathā pūrvaṃ tathā paścāt tasya kiṃ

ka
2b5 lpyate buddhaiḥ | pratītyotpadyate caiva pratītya ca
niΘrudhyate | ekasya sambhavo nāsti kathaṃ bālai vakal-
pyate | śaśagośṛṅgadṛṣṭāntaṃ ubhau kalpita(laka)

3a

above 1+1 **3a1** ṇau madhyamā pratipadyeya ⟨ta⟩thā sugatadharmmatā |
yathā caΘ(ndrārka)tārāṇāṃ svacche udakabhājana | dṛsyate
pratibimba hi tathā niṣpannalakṣaṇa⟨m*⟩ | ādimadhyān-
takalyāṇā(ṃ) a
3a2 visaṃvādakaṃ dhrūvaṃ | yasme caiṣaṃvidhānnātmā
katham āmtaΘti kalpyate | grīṣmakāl(e) yathā vāri uṣṇam ity
abidhīyate | tad eva sītakāleṣu sītam ity abidhīyate |
3a3 āvṛta kleśajālena cittam ity abidhīyate | tad eva Θ
(kle)śāpagamād bu(d)dha ity abhidhīyate | cakṣuḥ pratītya
rūpañ ca avabhāṣā sunirmalāḥ anutpannānirudhyat te dha
below 5+4 **3a4** (r)madhātuṃ prajānathaḥ | srotraṃ pratītya śabdas ca
cittavijñaΘptayaḥs trayaḥ | śrūyate svavikalpena dharma-
dhātur a‸⟨la⟩kṣaṇaḥ | ghrāṇaṃ gandhāsṛtaṃ ghrāṇi ārūpam
anidarśanaṃ |
below 5+5 **3a5** gh(r)āṇavijñānatathatā dharmadhātur vikalpyate | jihvā
svaΘbhāvā(s)ū(n)yā hi rasadhātur viviktatā | apratiṣṭhita-
vijñāna dharmadhātusvabhāvatā | suddha^{v}⟨ḥ⟩ kāyasvabhāvena

3b

3b1 sparṣapratyayalakṣaṇaṃ | pratyayebhyo vinirmukta
dhaΘrmadhātur vadāmy ahaṃ | sanaḥ pradhānadharmm(e)ṣu
kalpyākalpanavarjitaṃ | dharmmāṇāṃ nisvabhāvatna dhar-
madhātur vibhāvya
3b2 te | paśyate sṛṇute ghrāti svādate sparśatīti Θ (ca)
dharmāṃ vijānate yogī evaṃ niṣpannalakṣaṇaṃ | cakṣu sro-
traṃ ca ghrāṇañ ca jihvā kāyo manas tathā | ṣaḍāyatana
3b3 visuddhi {ga} etat tatvasya lakṣaṇaiḥ | cittam eta
dviΘdhā dṛṣṭa loki lokottarañ ca yat* | ātmagrāheṇa saṃsāre
pratyātma tathatā hi ta(dva$^{?}$) | rāgakṣayo hi nirvāṇa dve
3b4 ṣamohakayaś ca yat* | tasya bodhāya buddhatvaṃ

śaraΘṇaṃ sarvaṃ dehināṃ || asmi kaḍevare sarvaṃ jñānam ajñānam eva ca || badhyata svavikalpena mucyate svaparijñayāḥ |
3b5 bodhi na dūre nāsanne na gatā nāpi bhāgatā | na dṛśyaΘte dṛśyate caiva atraiva kleśapañ(j)are | uktañ ca sūtravarggeṣu viharaty ātmacintakaḥ | prajñādīpavihāreṇa

4a

ɔve 1+1 **4a1** paramā sāntim āgatāḥ na bodh(au) ^{v}⟨da⟩raṃ sajñī syān na (sā)|Θsanna saṃjñinam* | ṣaṇṇāṃ hi viṣayābhāsa yathābhūta(ṃ) pa(rijña)yā | yathodakeṇa sanmisraṃ kṣīram ekatra bhā
4a2 jane | kṣīraṃ pibanti haṃsā hi udakañ ca tathā sthitaṃ | Θ evaṃ hi kleśasanmisraṃ jñānam ekatra bhājane | pibanti yogino jñānaṃ ajñānaṃ sphorayanti te | ahaṃ mame
4a3 ti vā grāho yāvad bāhya vikalpyate | dṛṣṭe viṣayaΘnairātmyem bhavabījan nirudhyante | buddho hi pariṇirvvā sucir nityasubhālayaḥ | kalpayanti dvayaṃ bālār adva
4a4 yaṃ yogināṃ padaṃ | duṣkarair vividhair dānaiḥ | sīlais saΘtvārthasaṅgrahaiḥ | satvopakārakṣāṃtyā ca dhātupuṣṭir iyaṃ tridhā | vīryañ ca sarvadharmeṣu dhyāne ci pracāvratā ||
4a5 prajñāyām evaṇaṃ nityam bodhiṣuṣṭir iyam punaḥ | upāΘyasahitā prajñā praṇidhānair visodhitā | balesva susṭhita jñānaṃ dhātupuṣṭi caturdvidhā | (sa$^{?}$) bodhisatvā
4a6 (n t). vandeti atidurbhāṣitaṃ kṛtam* | bodhisatvam abīje tu Θ

4b

4b1 sannidhyaṃ tatra cintayet* | guḍaśarkkarakhaṇḍānāṃ uΘtpatti tatra jāya | rakṣite bodhicitte hi sānidhyan tatra cintayet* | arhatpratyekabuddhānāṃm utpatti tatra jāya
4b2 te | yathā śālyāṅkurādīnāṃ rakṣā kurvanti kārṣikāḥ Θ tathāśrayādhimuktānā rakṣā kurvantiṃ nāyakāḥ | yathā kṛṣṇacatu(r)dasyāṃ dṛsyate candravigraham* | tathāgrayānā
4b3 dhimuktānā dṛsyate buddhavigrahaṃ | yathaiva bālacandraΘsya dṛṣṭā vṛddhi kṣaṇe kṣaṇe | tathā bhūmipraviṣṭānā

dṛṣṭā vṛddhi kṣaṇe kṣaṇe | yathā hi pañcadasyāṃ vai pūrṇṇa-candro
4b4 hi jāyate | tathā niṣṭhāgatābhūmiṃ dharmakāyo hi jā-yaΘte | adhimuktidṛḍha yasya buddhe dharme ca nityasaḥ | utpādayati tac cittam anivartyam bhave bhave (kṛ)ṣṇāśraya-parā
below 5+5 **4b5** vṛttiḥ suklāśrayaparigraha | tadā tasyāvabodhena Θ mudi‸‹te›ty abhidhīyate | malinaṃ nityakāla(ṃ) hi rāgādyair vividhair malaiḥ | malābhāve ca yā suddhiḥ vimalety abhi

5a

5a1 dhīyate | nirodhoḥ kleśajālasya prabhābhrājaviniΘrmalā | apramāṇāndhakārasya vigatā tu prabhākarī | śuddhāḥ prab-hāsvarā nityaṃ saṅgajaiḥ parivajñitaṃ jñānārcci
5a2 ṣaiḥ parivṛtā bhūmir arcciṣmatī matī | sarvavidyāΘkalā-śilpadhyānānāñ ca vicitratā | durjaṣānā hi kleṣānā | vijayā tu sudurjaṣā | tisṛṇām api bodhīnāṃ
5a3 saṅgrahaṃ sarvasampadā | utpādavyayagambhītyā bhū-mis tv abhiΘmukhībhūtā | krīḍate raśmijālena cakravyūh(ai)s samantata | strīr l{..}(o?)kāt tārapaṅkaughair dūraṅgamā iti smṛtā | buddhais sa
5a4 tvāyamāṇo sau praviṣṭā jñānasāgare | anābhogavaΘsi-prāptaḥ akaṃpyā mārakiṅkaraiḥ | pratisaṃvitsu bharvāsu sa yogī pāramīgataḥ | dharmmadeśena sāṃka(thyai) bhūmi
5a5 (m*) sādhumatī smṛtā | kāya jñānamayaṃ rāmyaṃ ākāśam iΘva nirmala{{ḥ}}ṃ sandhārayati buddhānā dhar-mmameghāḥ samantatataḥ āśravaḥ sarvadharmmānā caryā-phalaparigrahaḥ

5b

5b1 āśrayasya parāvṛtti dharmmakāyo bidhīyate | acintyo Θ vāsanā muktasa cintyaḥ saṃsāravāsanaḥ tvam acintyo ṣi sarveṣāṃ ka(s tva) vijñātum arhasi | sarvavāg(v)iṣayā
5b2 t(ī)taṃ sarvendriyam agocaraṃ | manovijñānagamyo si Θ yo si yo si namo stu te | kramena samudrānītā buddhapu-trāḥ mahāyasā | dharmmameghena jñānena śūnyam paśyanti

dharmma
5b3 tāṃ | yadā prakṣālitaṃ cittaṃ uttīrṇ(ṇ)a bhavasāgarān* | Θ mahāpadmamayan tasya āsanaṃ sampratiṣṭhati | anekaratnapatrābhaṃ lakṣaṇaujvalakalpikāṃ | anekaiḥ padma
5b4 k(o)ṭībhiḥ samantāt parivāritam* | daśabhiś ca balair bāΘla tiṣṭhate bālacandravat* | klesair malinasattānaṃ na pasyati tathāgataḥ yadā pretāḥ samantā tu suṣkāṃ pasyanti
5b5 [1] Θ sāgaraḥ tathaivājñānadagdhānā buddho nāstīti kalpanā | satvānātm aṃlpapuṇyānā bhagavāṅ kiṅ kariṣyantiḥ jāty(a)

[1] Line 5 begins only after the string-hole because the palm leaf is too narrow before it. The Tibetan words (in *dbu med* script) *bstod pa 'dra na tshogs naṅ* have been written in the narrow area.

Critical Edition

(1a1) dharmadhāto[1, 2] namas tubhyaṃ
sarvasattveṣv avasthita |
yasya te aparijñānād[3]
bhramanti tribhavālaye || <1>

ya eva dhātuḥ[4] saṃsāre
śodhyamānaḥ[5] sa eva (1a2) tu |
śuddhaḥ sa eva nirvāṇe
dharmakāyaḥ[6] sa eva hi || <2>

yathā hi kṣīrasammiśraṃ[7]
sarpimaṇḍaṃ na dṛśyate |
tathā hi kleśasammiśro[8]
dharmadhātur na dṛśyate || <3>

yathā vi(1a3)śodhitaṃ kṣīraṃ
ghṛtadravyaṃ sunirmalam[9] |
tathā viśodhitāḥ[10] kleśā
dharmadhātuḥ[11] sunirmalaḥ || <4>

yathā dīpo ghaṭastho hi
na kiñcid avabhāsate |
tathā kleśaghaṭa(1a4)stho hi
dharmadhātur na bhāsate[12] || <5>

---

[1] *dharmadhāto* em. : *dharmmadhātuḥ* Ms

[2] 法身 Ch1 for *dharmadhātuṃ*

[3] In order to avoid the hiatus *te aparijñānād*, this could be corrected into *te hy aparijñānād* or *te te 'parijñānād*. However the text is likely acceptable here. For other instances of hiatuses in this text, see below 11c, 14d.

[4] *rgyur gyur pa* T, 性 Ch1 for *dhātuḥ*

[5] *śodhyamānaḥ* em. : *śodhyamānya* Ms

[6] *dharmakāyaḥ* em. : *dharmmakāya* Ms

[7] *kṣīrasammiśraṃ* em. : *kṣīrasamiśraṃ* Ms

[8] *kleśasammiśro* em. : *kleśasanmiśraṃ* Ms

[9] *sunirmalaṃ* em. (*sunirmalaḥ* 4d) : *sanirmmalaṃ* Ms

[10] *viśodhitāḥ* em. : *visodhitā* Ms

[11] *dharma*° em. : *dharmā*° Ms

[12] *mthoṅ* T for *bhāsate*

yena yena hi pārśvena
cchidrībhavati tad ghaṭam |
tena tena hi pārśvena
raśmayas[13] tasya nirgatāḥ[14] || <6>

yadā samādhivajreṇa
bhinnaṃ bhavati (1a5) tad ghaṭam |
sa tadākāśaparyantaṃ[15]
samantād avabhāsate || <7>

dharmadhātur na cotpanno[16]
na niruddhaḥ[17] kadācana[18] |
sarvakālam asaṅkliṣṭa[19]
ādimadhyāntanirmalaḥ || <8>

yathā vaiḍūrya(1b1)ratnaṃ hi
sarvakālaprabhāsvaram |
pāṣāṇakośe sañchannam[20]
ābhā tasya na rājate || <9>

evaṃ hi kleśasañchanno
dharmadhātuḥ sunirmalaḥ[21] |
nāsau[22] bhrājati saṃsāre
nirvāṇe (1b2) tu[23] prabhāsvaraḥ || <10>

gotre ca sati[24] vyāyāmo[25]

---

13 *raśmayas* em. : *rasmaya* Ms ◦ *'od kyi raṅ bzin* T = **raśmayas* for *raśmayas*

14 *nirgatāḥ* em. : *nirgatā* Ms

15 °*paryantaṃ* em. : °*paryanta* Ms

16 *cotpanno* em. : *cotpannā* Ms

17 *niruddhaḥ* em.: *niruddhā* Ms

18 *kadācana* em. : *kadācanaṃ* Ms

19 *asaṅkliṣṭa* em. : *asaṃkliṣṭhaṃ* Ms

20 *sañchannam* em. : *saṃcchanna* Ms

21 *su*° em. (*śin tu* T) : *sa*° Ms

22 *nāsau* em. : *nāso* Ms

23 *tu* conj. : *tat* Ms

24 *ca sati* em. (*yod na* T, 有 Ch1) : (*vā satti*?) Ms

25 *vyāyāmo* em. (有功 Ch1): *vyāyāma* Ms ◦ *las byas pas* T = **vyāyāmāj* for

jātarūpanidarśanāt[26] |
gotre asati vyāyāmaḥ[27]
śramaḥ kevalam iṣyate || <11>

yathā[28] hi tuṣasañchannaṃ[29]
na dhānyaṃ tat phalaṃ matam[30] |
(1b3) tathā hi kleśasañchanno
nāsau buddheti[31] kalpyate || <12>

yathā hi tuṣanirmuktaṃ
tat phalaṃ pratibhāsate |
tathā hi kleśanirmukto
dharmakāyaḥ[32] prabhāsate[33] || <13>

upamā[34] kriyate loke (1b4)
kadalyā nāsti sāratā[35] |
phalāni tasya sārāṇi
bhakṣyate amṛtopamā[36] || <14>

evaṃ hy asāre saṃsāre[37]
nirvṛte[38] kleśasāgare[39] |

---

vyāyāmo

[26] *mthoṅ bar 'gyur* T = *°*darśanam* for °*darśanāt*

[27] *vyāyāmaḥ* em. (有功 Ch1) : *vyāyāma* Ms ◦ *las byas na* T = **vyāyāme* for *vyāyāmaḥ*

[28] *yathā* em. : *ahaṃ yathā* Ms

[29] °*sañchannaṃ* conj. (°*sañchanno* 12c, *g.yogs pas* T, 覆其上 Ch1, 纏裹 Ch2) : °*gacchantaṃ* Ms

[30] *matam* em. : *mataḥ* Ms

[31] *buddheti* em. (*saṅs rgyas* T, 佛 Ch1) : *byaddheti* Ms

[32] *dharmakāyaḥ* em.: *dharmakāya* Ms

[33] *prabhāsate* em. (13b, *rab tu gsal* T, 顯現 Ch1, 顯 Ch2) : *ṣrabhāvyate* Ms

[34] *upa<mā>* em. (*dper* T, 譬喻 Ch1) : *upa* Ms

[35] *sāratā* em. : *sārata* Ms

[36] *amṛtopamā* em. (如甘露 Ch1) : *amṛtopamāḥ* Ms ◦ *mṅar po … ltar* T for *amṛtopamā*

[37] *saṃsāre* em. : *sāsāre* Ms

[38] 流轉 Ch1 = **nirvṛtte* for *nirvṛte*

[39] *gzeb* T = *pañjare* (°*pañjare* 49d) for *sāgare*

phalaṃ tasyāpi buddhatvam[40]
amṛtaṃ sarvade(1b5)hinām[41] || <15>

evaṃ hi sarvabījeṣu[42]
sādṛśyaṃ jāyate phalam |
bījair[43] vinā phalaṃ nāsti
kaḥ[44] prājñaḥ pratipatsyate[45] || <16>

bījabhūtas tv asau[46] dhātur
dharmāṇām[47] āśrayo mataḥ |
śodhyamā(2a1)naḥ[48] krameṇaivaṃ[49]
buddhatvāspadam[50] āvahet || <17>

nirmalau[51] candrasūryau hi
āvṛtau pañcabhir malaiḥ |
abhranīhāradhūmena
rāhuvaktrarajādibhiḥ[52] || <18>[53]

evaṃ prabhāsvaraṃ cittam
ā(2a2)vṛtaṃ[54] pañcabhir malaiḥ |
kāmavyāpādamiddhena[55]
auddhatyavicikitsayā[56] || <19>

---

[40] 佛體 Ch1 = **buddhakāyaḥ* for *buddhatvam*

[41] 施有施 Ch1 = **deyānāṃ dehi* for *sarvadehinām*

[42] °*bījeṣu* em. (*sa bon* T, 種 Ch1) : °*jīveṣu* Ms

[43] *bījair* em. (*sa bon* T, 種 Ch1) : *jīvair* Ms

[44] *kaḥ* em. : *ka* Ms

[45] *pratipatsyate* em. : *pratipatsyete* Ms

[46] *bījabhūtas tv asau* em. : *bījabhūtas tasau* Ms

[47] *dharmāṇām* em. : *dharmānām* Ms

[48] *śodhyamānaḥ* em. : *śodhyamāna* Ms

[49] om. T, Ch1 for *evaṃ*

[50] *buddhatvāspadam* em. : *buddhatvaspadam* Ms

[51] *nirmalau* em. (SUṬ) : *nirmālau* Ms

[52] °*vaktra*° (*gdoṅ* T) : 手 Ch1 ◦ °*rajomalaiḥ* SUṬ for *rajādibhiḥ*

[53] Stanzas 18-23, cited in Nāropā's SUṬ.

[54] *āvṛtaṃ* em. : *āvṛttaṃ* Ms

[55] °*middhena* em. (SUṬ) : °*mithyena* Ms

agniśaucaṃ yathā vastraṃ
malinaṃ[57] vividhair malaiḥ |
agnimadhye yathā kṣiptaṃ
malaṃ dagdhaṃ na va(2a3)stratā || <20>

evaṃ prabhāsvaraṃ cittaṃ
malinaṃ rāgajair malaiḥ |
jñānāgninā malaṃ dagdhaṃ
na dagdhaṃ[58] tat prabhāsvaram || <21>

śūnyatāhārakāḥ[59] sūtrā[60]
ye kecid bhāṣitā jinaiḥ[61] |
sarvais taiḥ (2a4) kleśavyāvṛttir[62]
naiva dhātor vināśanam || <22>

pṛthivyantarhitaṃ[63] toyaṃ
yathā tiṣṭhati nirmalam[64] |
kleśair antaritaṃ jñānaṃ
tathābhāti sunirmalam[65] || <23>

dharmadhātur[66] yato[67] nātmā[68]
na (2a5) ca strīnṛnapuṃsakaḥ[69] |

---

[56] *auddhatyavicikitsayā* em. (SUṬ) : *audhatyaṃvicikiṃtsayā* Ms

[57] *malinaṃ* em. (SUṬ) : *malina* Ms

[58] *dagdhaṃ* em.: *ddhagdhaṃ* Ms

[59] °*āhārakāḥ* em. : °*āhārakā* Ms

[60] *sūtrā* em. (SUṬ, *mdo* T, 契經 Ch1) : *subhrāḥ* Ms

[61] 如來 Ch1 = **tathāgataiḥ*, 世尊 Ch2 = **bhagavadbhiḥ* for *jinaiḥ*

[62] *sarvais taiḥ kleśavyāvṛttir* em. (SUṬ, *de dag kun gyis* T) : *sarvās tāḥ kleśavyāvṛttī* Ms

[63] °*antarhitaṃ* em. : °*āntarhitān* Ms

[64] *nirmalam* em. : *nirrmalam* Ms

[65] *tiṣṭhati nirmalam* SUṬ, *dri ma med par gnas* T for *tathābhāti sunirmalam*

[66] °*dhātur* em. (*dbyiṅs* T, 界 Ch1, Ch2) : °*dhāpu* Ms

[67] *yato* em. (*gaṅ phyir* T) : *yadā*° Ms

[68] 無我 Ch2 = **anātmā* for *nātmā*

[69] °*nṛnapuṃsakaḥ* em. (二形及女男 Ch2) : °*nanapuṃsakaṃ* Ms ◦ *bud med ma yin skyes pa min* T, 非女亦非男 Ch1 for *strīnṛnapuṃsakaḥ*

sarvagrāhavinirmuktaḥ[70]
katham ātmeti[71] kalpyate || <24>

(2b1) sarve[72] dharmā hy asaṃsaktāḥ
strīpuṃstvaṃ[73] hi na vidyate |
rāgāndhavineyārthāya[74]
strīpuṃstvaṃ[75] hi[76] pradarśitam || <25>

anityaduḥkhaśūnyeti[77]
cittanidhyaptayas[78] trayaḥ |
paramā cittani(2b2)dhyaptir[79]
dharmāṇāṃ[80] niḥsvabhāvatā[81] || <26>

yathā hi garbho garbhiṇyāṃ
vidyate na ca dṛśyate |
tathā hi kleśasañchannaṃ
dharmatattvaṃ[82] na dṛśyate || <27>

caturṇāṃ hi vikalpānām[83]
utpattir bhūtabhau(2b3)tikāt[84] |
ahaṃmamavikalpo hi[85]

---

[70] °*nirmuktaḥ* em. : °*nirmuktaṃ* Ms

[71] *ātmeti* em. : *āmmeti* Ms

[72] *sarve* em. : *savva* Ms

[73] °*puṃstvaṃ* Ms^{pc} (*skyes pa* T, 男 Ch1) : °*ṣuṃstvaṃ* Ms^{ac}

[74] *rāgāndhavineyārthāya* em. (*'dod chags kyis ldoṅs gdul bya'i phyir* D : *'dod chags kyis gduṅs gdul bya'i phyir* CGNP, 貪盲調伏故 Ch1) : *rāgātvavinayārthāya* Ms

[75] °*puṃstvaṃ* em. : °*pustvaṃ* Ms

[76] *hi* em. (*hi* 25b) : om. Ms

[77] °*duḥkha*° em. : °*duḥkhaṃ* Ms

[78] *cittanidhyaptayas* em. : *cittanidhyaptayaḥs* Ms

[79] *nidhyaptir* em. : *nidhyapti* Ms

[80] *dharmāṇāṃ* em. : *dharmāṇā* Ms

[81] *niḥsvabhāvatā* em. : *nisvabhāvatā* Ms

[82] °*tattvaṃ* em. (實 Ch1) : °*tātvaṃ* Ms ◦ *dbyiṅs* T, 界 Ch2 = **dhātur* for °*tattvaṃ*

[83] *vikalpānām* em. : *vikalpāṇām* Ms

[84] °*bhautikāt* em. (*'byuṅ las* T) : °*bhautikā* Ms^{pc} : °*bhaukā* Ms^{ac}

nāmasañjñānimittajaḥ[86] || <28>

praṇidhānaṃ[87] hi buddhānāṃ[88]
nirābhāsam alakṣaṇam[89] |
pratyātmavedyayogitvād[90]
buddhānāṃ[91] nityadharmatā || <29>

yathā śaśaviṣā(2b4)ṇaṃ[92] hi
kalpyamānaṃ[93] na vidyate |
tathā hi sarvadharmeṣu
kalpitaṃ[94] naiva vidyate || <30>

paramāṇurajaḥ[95] kintu
goviṣāṇaṃ[96] na vidyate |
yathā pūrvaṃ tathā paścāt
tasya[97] kiṃ ka(2b5)lpyate budhaiḥ[98] || <31>

pratītyotpadyate caiva
pratītya ca nirudhyate |
ekasya sambhavo nāsti
kathaṃ bālair vikalpyate[99] || <32>

---

85 *hi* em. : *ti* Ms

86 °*nimittajaḥ* em. (*rgyu mtshan gyis* T) : °*nimittājaṃ* Ms ∘ 名想及境界 Ch2 = **nāma sañjñā nimittaṃ ca* for *nāmasañjñānimittajaḥ*

87 *praṇidhānaṃ* em. : *pranidhāna* Ms

88 *buddhānāṃ* em. : *buddhāṇāṃ* Ms

89 *alakṣaṇam* em. : *alakṣaṇām* Ms

90 *pratyātmavedyayogitvād* em. (*raṅ rig sbyor ldan ñid* T, 自覺相應故 Ch1) : *pratyātmayogitvād* Ms ∘ *raṅ rig sbyor ldan ñid* T = **pratyātmavedyayogitvaṃ* for *pratyātmavedyayogitvād*

91 *buddhānāṃ* em. : *buddhāṇāṃ* Ms

92 °*viṣāṇaṃ* em. : °*viṣāṇā* Ms

93 *kalpyamānaṃ* em. : *kalpyamāna* Ms. ∘ *btags pa* CGNP for *kalpyamānaṃ*

94 *btags pa* CGNP for *kalpitaṃ*

95 *paramāṇu*° em. : *paramānu*° Ms

96 °*viṣāṇaṃ* em. (*rwa* T) : °*vidvānaṃ* Ms ∘ 分別 Ch1 = **kalpitaṃ* for *goviṣāṇaṃ*

97 *de la* T = **tasmin* for *tasya*

98 *budhaiḥ* em. (智 Ch1) : *buddhaiḥ* Ms ∘ om. T for *budhaiḥ*

99 *bālair vikalpyate* em. : *bālai vakalpyate* Ms

śaśagośṛṅgadṛṣṭāntam
ubhau kalpitalakṣa(3a1)ṇau[100] |
madhyamā[101] pratipadyeta
yathā[102] sugatadharmatā || <33>

yathā candrārkatārāṇāṃ
svaccha[103] udakabhājane[104] |
dṛśyate pratibimbaṃ[105] hi
tathā niṣpannalakṣaṇam || <34>

ādimadhyāntakalyāṇam[106]
a(3a2)visaṃvādakaṃ dhruvam[107] |
yasya[108] caivaṃvidhānātmā[109, 110]
katham ātmeti[111] kalpyate || <35>

grīṣmakāle yathā vāri
uṣṇam ity abhidhīyate[112] |
tad eva śītakāleṣu
śītam ity abhidhīyate[113] || <36>

(3a3) āvṛtaṃ[114] kleśajālena
cittam[115] ity abhidhīyate[116] |

---

100 om. T for *ubhau kalpitalakṣaṇau*

101 *madhyamā* : *dbu ma ñid du* T, 於中道 Ch1 = **madhyamāyāṃ* for *madhyamā*

102 *pratipadyeta yathā* em. (*ji ltar … sgrub par byed* T, 依住 … 如 Ch1) : *pratipadye yathā* Ms^{ac} : *pratipadyeya tathā* Ms^{pc}

103 *svaccha* em. : *svacche* Ms

104 °*bhājane* em. : °*bhājana* Ms

105 *pratibimbaṃ* em. : *pratibimba* Ms

106 °*kalyāṇam* em. : °*kalyāṇāṃ* Ms

107 *dhruvam* em. : *dhrūvaṃ* Ms

108 *yasya* em. : *yasme* Ms

109 *caivaṃ*° em. (*de ltar* T) : *caiṣaṃ*° Ms ◦ 五(種) Ch1 = **pañca*(*vidha*) for *caivaṃ*

110 *vidhānā*° em. : *vidhānnā*° Ms

111 *ātmeti* em. : *āmtati* Ms

112 *abhidhīyate* em. (*abhidhīyate* 37d, *brjod par byed* T, 名 Ch1) : *abidhīyate* Ms

113 *abhidhīyate* em. : *abidhīyate* Ms

114 *āvṛtaṃ* em. : *āvṛta* Ms

tad eva kleśāpagamād
buddha ity abhidhīyate || <37>

cakṣuḥ pratītya rūpaṃ ca
avabhāsāḥ[117] sunirmalāḥ |
anutpannāniruddhās[118] te
dha(3a4)rmadhātuṃ prajānatha[119] || <38>

śrotraṃ pratītya śabdaṃ ca[120]
cittaṃ[121] vijñaptayas[122] trayaḥ |
śrūyate svavikalpena[123]
dharmadhātur alakṣaṇaḥ || <39>

ghrāṇaṃ gandhāśritaṃ[124] ghrāṇi[125]
arūpam[126] anidarśanam[127] |
(3a5) ghrāṇavijñānatathatā[128]
dharmadhātur vikalpyate || <40>

jihvā svabhāvaśūnyā[129] hi
rasadhātur viviktatā[130] |

---

[115] *sems can* T = **sattvam* for *cittam*

[116] *abhidhīyate* em. : *abidhīyate* Ms

[117] *avabhāsāḥ* em. : *avabhāṣā* Ms

[118] °*niruddhās* conj. : °*nirudhyat* Ms

[119] *prajānatha* em. : *prajānathaḥ* Ms

[120] *śabdaṃ ca* em. : *śabdas ca* Ms

[121] *cittaṃ* em. : *citta*° Ms

[122] *vijñaptayas* em. : *vijñaptayaḥs* Ms ◦ *rnam par dag pa'i śes pa* T, 清淨識 Ch1 = **viśuddhajñaptayas* for *cittaṃ vijñaptayas*

[123] *rtog daṅ bcas pas* T = **savikalpena* for *svavikalpena*

[124] °*āśritaṃ* em. : °*āsṛtaṃ* Ms

[125] *snom* T, 嗅 Ch1 = **ghrāti* for *ghrāṇi ārūpam* Ms

[126] *arūpam* em. : *ārūpam* Ms. I assume that the Sanskrit word *ārūpam* here in the MS is an equivalent of the more common *arūpam*. It is worth noting that *ārūpa* as a synonym of *ārūpya* (adjective and noun) is attested in the Buddhist Sanskrit (cf. BHSD: *s.v.*).

[127] *gzugs su med pa'i dpe* T = **arūpanidarśanam* for *arūpam anidarśanam*

[128] *de bźin sna yi rnam śes kyis* T = **tathā ghrāṇavijñānena*, 鼻識是真如 Ch1 = **ghrāṇavijñānaṃ tathatā* for *ghrāṇavijñānatathatā*

[129] *svabhāva*° em. : *svabhāvā*° Ms

apratiṣṭhitavijñānaṃ[131]
dharmadhātusvabhāvatā[132] || <41>

śuddhakāyasvabhāvena[133] (3b1)
sparśapratyayalakṣaṇam |
pratyayebhyo vinirmuktaṃ[134]
dharmadhātuṃ[135] vadāmy aham[136] || <42>

manaḥ[137] pradhānadharmeṣu
kalpyakalpanavarjitam[138] |
dharmāṇāṃ niḥsvabhāvatvaṃ[139]
dharmadhātur vibhāvya(3b2)te[140] || <43>

paśyate śṛṇute ghrāti
svādate spṛśatīti[141] ca |
dharmān vijānate yogī
evaṃ niṣpannalakṣaṇam || <44>

cakṣuḥ[142] śrotraṃ ca ghrāṇaṃ ca
jihvā kāyo manas tathā |
ṣaḍāyatanaṃ[143] (3b3) viśuddham[144]
etat tattvasya lakṣaṇam[145] || <45>

---

130 *kyaṅ dben pa ste* = **vivikto 'pi* for *viviktatā*

131 °*vijñānaṃ* em. : °*vijñāna* Ms ◦ 無依亦無識 Ch1 = **apratiṣṭhitāvijñānaṃ* for *apratiṣṭhitavijñānaṃ*

132 *ṅo bo yis* CGNP, 自性故 Ch1 = **svabhāvatvāt* for °*svabhāvatā*

133 *śuddha* em. : *śuddha‹ḥ›*° Ms

134 *vinirmuktaṃ* em. : *vinirmukta* Ms

135 *dharmadhātuṃ* em. : *dharmadhātur* Ms

136 om. T for *aham*

137 *manaḥ* em. : *sanaḥ* Ms

138 *kalpya*° em. : *kalpyā*° Ms

139 *niḥsvabhāvatvaṃ* em. : *nisvabhāvatna* Ms

140 分別 Ch1 = **vikalpyate* for *vibhāvyate*

141 *spṛśatīti* em. : *sparśatīti* Ms

142 *cakṣuḥ* em. : *cakṣu* Ms

143 *ṣaḍāyatanaṃ* em. : *ṣaḍāyatana* Ms

144 *viśuddham* em.: *viśuddhi* {*ga*} Ms

145 *lakṣaṇam* em. (*'di ñid de ñid mtshan ñid do* T, 如是彼之相 Ch1) : *lakṣaṇaiḥ*

cittam eva[146] dvidhā dṛṣṭaṃ[147]
loki lokottaraṃ ca yat |
ātmagrāheṇa saṃsāraḥ[148]
pratyātma[149] tathatā hi tat[150] || <46>

rāgakṣayo[151] hi nirvāṇaṃ[152]
dve(3b4)ṣamohakṣayaś ca yat |[153]
tasya bodhāya[154] buddhatvaṃ[155]
śaraṇaṃ sarvadehinām[156] || <47>

asmiṃ[157] kalevare[158] sarvaṃ
jñānam ajñānam eva ca |
badhyate[159] svavikalpena
mucyate svaparijñayā[160] || <48>

(3b5) bodhir[161] na dūre nāsanne
na gatā nāpi vāgatā[162] |
na dṛśyate dṛśyate caiva[163]

Ms

[146] *eva* em. (*ñid* T) : *eta* Ms

[147] *dṛṣṭaṃ* em. (*mthoṅ* D : *mtho* CGNP, 見 Ch1) : *dṛṣṭa* Ms

[148] *saṃsāraḥ* em. (*'khor ba ste* T, 為流轉 Ch1) : *saṃsāre* Ms

[149] *so sor rig* T, 自覺 Ch1 for *pratyātma*

[150] *tat* em. = *ta*(*dva*?) Ms

[151] 無盡 Ch1 = **akṣayo* for *rāgakṣayo*

[152] *nirvāṇaṃ* em. : *nirvāṇa* Ms

[153] 無盡是涅槃 若盡貪及癡 Ch1 for *rāgakṣayo hi nirvāṇaṃ dveṣamohakṣayaś ca yat*

[154] *'gags pas* T = **rodhena*, 覺 Ch1 = **bodhati* for *bodhāya*

[155] 佛體 Ch1 = **buddhakāyaḥ* for *buddhatvaṃ*

[156] *sarva*° em. : *sarvaṃ* Ms

[157] *asmiṃ* em. : *asmi* Ms

[158] *kalevare* em. : *kaḍevare* Ms

[159] *badhyate* em. : *badhyata* Ms

[160] °*parijñayā* em. : °*parijñayāḥ* Ms

[161] *bodhir* em. : *bodhi* Ms

[162] *vāgatā* em. (*'oṅ ba'aṅ* T, 來 Ch1) : *bhāgatā* Ms

[163] 壞滅及顯現 Ch1 for *na dṛśyate dṛśyate ca*

atraiva kleśapañjare || <49>

uktaṃ ca sūtravargeṣu
viharaty[164] ātmacintakaḥ |
prajñādīpavihāreṇa (4a1)
paramāṃ[165] śāntim āgataḥ[166] || <50>

na bodher dūraṃ[167] sañjñī[168] syān
na sāsannā ca[169] sañjñinaḥ[170] |
ṣaṇṇāṃ hi viṣayābhāso[171]
yathābhūtaṃ parijñayā || <51> [61]

yathodakena[172] sammiśraṃ
kṣīram ekatra bhā(4a2)jane |
kṣīraṃ pibanti haṃsā hi
udakaṃ ca tathā sthitam || <52> [62]

evaṃ hi kleśasammiśraṃ
jñānam ekatra bhājane[173] |
pibanti[174] yogino jñānam
ajñānaṃ[175] sphorayanti te || <53> [63]

ahaṃ mame(4a3)ti vā grāho
yāvad bāhyo[176] vikalpyate |
dṛṣṭe viṣayanairātmye[177]

---

[164] *gnas bya źes* T for *viharaty*

[165] *paramāṃ* em. : *paramā* Ms

[166] *āgataḥ* em. : *āgatāḥ* Ms

[167] *bodher dūraṃ* conj. : *bodhau ‹da›raṃ* Ms

[168] *sañjñī* em. : *sajñī* Ms

[169] *sāsannā ca* conj. (*yaṅ* T, 亦 Ch1) : *sāsanna* Ms

[170] *sañjñinaḥ* em. : *saṃjñinam* Ms

[171] *viṣayābhāso* em. : *viṣayābhāsa* Ms

[172] °*odakena* em. : °*odakeṇa* Ms

[173] *lus 'dir* T for *bhājane*

[174] *len* T for *pibanti*

[175] 煩惱 Ch1 = **kleśaṃ* for *ajñānaṃ*

[176] *bāhyo* em. : *bāhya* Ms

[177] °*nairātmye* em. : °*nairātmyem* Ms ◦ *bdag med rnam pa gñis* T, 二無我 Ch1 =

bhavabījaṃ nirudhyate[178] || <54> [64]

buddho hi parinirvāti[179]
śucir nityaśubhālayaḥ[180] |
kalpayanti[181] dvayaṃ bālā[182]
adva(4a4)yaṃ yogināṃ padam[183] || <55> [65]

duṣkarair vividhair dānaiḥ
śīlaiḥ sattvārthasaṅgrahaiḥ |
sattvopakārakṣāntyā[184] ca
dhātupuṣṭir iyaṃ tridhā || <56> [66]

vīryaṃ ca sarvadharmeṣu
dhyāne cittaṃ pracāritam[185] |
(4a5) prajñāyām acalaṃ[186] nityaṃ
bodhipuṣṭir[187] iyaṃ punaḥ || <57> [67]

upāyasahitā prajñā
praṇidhānair viśodhitā |
baleṣu[188] suṣṭhitaṃ[189] jñānaṃ
dhātupuṣṭiś caturvidhā[190] || <58> [68]

mā[191] bodhisattvā(4a6)n tu[192] vandeti

**dvividhanairātmye* for *viṣayanairātmye*

178 *nirudhyate* em. : *nirudhyante* Ms

179 °*parinirvā<ti>* em. : *pariṇirvvā* Ms

180 無垢 Ch1 = **nirmala* for *ālayaḥ*

181 *btags* GNP, *gtags* C for *kalpayanti*

182 *bālā* em. : *bālār* Ms

183 句 Ch1 for *padam*

184 一切損 Ch1 = **sarvāpakāra*° for *sattvopakāra*°

185 *ci<ttaṃ> pracāritam* em. (*sems 'jug pa* T, 心加行 Ch1) : *ci pracāvratā* Ms

186 *acalaṃ* em. (*brtan pa* CGNP : *bstan pa* D, 習 Ch1) : *evaṇaṃ* Ms

187 °*puṣṭir* em. : °*ṣuṣir* Ms

188 *baleṣu* em. : *balesva* Ms

189 *suṣṭhitaṃ* em.: *suṣṭhita* Ms

190 *dhātupuṣṭiś caturvidhā* em.: *dhātupuṣṭi caturdvidhā* Ms

191 *mā* em. (*mi bya* T, 不應 Ch1) : (*sa*$^{?}$) Ms

192 *tu* em. : *t.* Ms

atidurbhāṣitaṃ kṛtam |
bodhisattvam ajīvaṃ[193] tu
(4b1) xxxx⏑–⏑x || <59> [69]

xxxx⏑—x
xxxx⏑–⏑x |
xxxx⏑—x
xxxx⏑–⏑x || <60> [70]

xxxx⏑—x[194]
sannidhāyātra[195] cintayet[196] |
guḍaśarkarakhaṇḍānām
utpattis tatra jāyate[197] || <61> [71]

rakṣite bodhicitte hi
sannidhāyātra[198] cintayet[199] |
arhatpratyekabuddhānām
utpattis tatra jāya(4b2)te || <62> [72]

yathā śālyāṅkurādīnāṃ[200]
rakṣāṃ[201] kurvanti kārṣikāḥ |
tathāśrayādhimuktānāṃ[202]

---

193 *ajīvaṃ* em. (*ma byuṅ bar* T) : *abīje* Ms ∘ 不親 Ch1 for *ajīvaṃ*

194 Ms lacks six *pāda*s, 59d, 60a-d and 71a, according to T and Ch1, 59d = **dharmakāyo na jāyate* (*chos kyi sku ni 'byuṅ ma yin* T, 不生其法身 Ch1), 60 = **ikṣubījaṃ hi dviṣṭe yaḥ śarkarāṃ sa bubhukṣate* | *abhavaty ikṣubīje hi śarkarāpi na jāyate* || (*bur śiṅ sa bon la sdaṅ gaṅ* || *kha ra spyad par 'dod pa des* || *bur śiṅ sa bon med par ni* || *kha ra 'byuṅ bar 'gyur ma yin* || T, 憎於甘蔗種 欲食於石蜜 若壞甘蔗種 無由石蜜生 Ch1), 61a = **rakṣita ikṣubīje hi* (*rakṣite bodhicitte hi* 62a, *bur śiṅ sa bon gaṅ bsruṅs nas* T, 若護甘蔗種 Ch1)

195 *sannidhāyātra* em. (*ñe bar gnas śiṅ* T) : *sannidhyaṃ tatra* Ms ∘ om. Ch1 for *sannidhāyātra*

196 *bsgrubs pa* T, 可得 Ch1 for *cintayet*

197 *jāyate* em. (*jāyate*, 62d, *'g yur ba* T, 必得生 Ch1) : *jāya* Ms

198 *sannidhāyātra* em. (*ñe bar gnas śiṅ* T) : *sānidhyan tatra* Ms ∘ om. Ch1 for *sannidhāyātra*

199 *bsgrubs pa* T, 可得 Ch1 for *cintayet*

200 *sā lu'i sa bon sogs* T for *śālyāṅkurādīnāṃ*

201 *rakṣāṃ* em. : *rakṣā* Ms

202 *theg mchog* T = * °*agrayāna*° (maybe eye skip to [74c]) for °*āśraya*°, om. Ch1

rakṣāṃ[203] kurvanti[204] nāyakāḥ[205] || <63> [73]

yathā kṛṣṇacaturdaśyāṃ
dṛśyate candravigraham |
tathāgrayānā(4b3)dhimuktānāṃ[206]
dṛśyate buddhavigraham || <64> [74]

yathaiva bālacandrasya
dṛṣṭā vṛddhiḥ[207] kṣaṇe kṣaṇe |
tathā bhūmipraviṣṭānāṃ[208]
dṛṣṭā vṛddhiḥ[209] kṣaṇe kṣaṇe[210] || <65> [75]

yathā hi pañcadaśyāṃ vai
pūrṇacandro (4b4) hi jāyate |
tathā niṣṭhāgatābhūmyāṃ[211]
dharmakāyo hi jāyate[212] || <66> [76]

adhimuktidṛḍhaṃ[213] yasya
buddhe dharme[214] ca nityaśaḥ |
utpādayati tac cittam
anivartyam bhave bhave || <67> [77]

kṛṣṇāśrayaparā(4b5)vṛttiḥ
śuklāśrayaparigrahaḥ[215] |

◦ °*muktānāṃ* em. : °*muktānā* Ms

[203] *rakṣāṃ* em. : *rakṣā* Ms

[204] *kurvanti* em. : *kurvantiṃ* Ms

[205] 如來 Ch1 = **tathāgatāḥ* for *nāyakāḥ*

[206] om. Ch1 for °*agrayāna*° (*theg mchog* T) : ◦ °*muktānāṃ* em. : °*muktānā* Ms

[207] *vṛddhiḥ* em. : *vṛddhi* Ms

[208] °*praviṣṭānāṃ* em. : °*praviṣṭānā* Ms

[209] *vṛddhiḥ* em. : *vṛddhi* Ms

[210] *rim gyis rim gyis* T = **krame krame*, 念念 Ch1 = **citte citte* for *kṣaṇe kṣaṇe*

[211] °*āgatābhūmyāṃ* em. : °*āgatābhūmiṃ* Ms

[212] *rdzogs śiṅ gsal* T, 顯(法身 法身)理無缺 Ch2 for *jāyate*

[213] *adhimuktidṛḍhaṃ* em.: *adhimuktidṛḍha* Ms

[214] *saṅs rgyas chos daṅ dge 'dun la* T = **buddhe dharme saṅghe ca* for *buddhe dharme*

[215] °*parigrahaḥ* em. : °*parigraha* Ms

tadā tasyāvabodhena
muditety abhidhīyate || <68> [78]

malinaṃ nityakālaṃ hi
rāgādyair vividhair malaiḥ |
malābhāve ca yā śuddhiḥ
vimalety abhi(5a1)dhīyate || <69> [79]

nirodhāt[216] kleśajālasya
prabhābhrājavinirmalā[217] |
apramāṇāndhakārasya
vigatā tu prabhākarī || <70> [80]

śuddhā[218] prabhāsvarā nityaṃ
saṅgajaiḥ[219] parivarjitā[220] |
jñānārci(5a2)ṣaiḥ parivṛtā
bhūmir arciṣmatī matā[221] || <71> [81]

sarvavidyākalāśilpa-
dhyānānāṃ ca vicitratā |
durjayānāṃ[222] hi kleśānāṃ[223]
vijayā tu sudurjayā[224] || <72> [82]

tisṛṇām api bodhīnāṃ (5a3)
saṅgrahaḥ[225] sarvasampadām[226] |
utpādavyayagambhīrā[227]
bhūmis tv abhimukhībhūtā || <73> [83]

---

[216] *nirodhāt* em. (*'gags nas* T) : *nirodhoḥ* Ms

[217] *śes rab* T = **prajñā* for °*bhrāja*°

[218] *śuddhā* em. : *śuddhāḥ* Ms

[219] *'du 'dzi* T = **saṃsargaiḥ*, 世吉祥 Ch1 = **sargaśrībhiḥ* for *saṅgajaiḥ*

[220] *parivarjitā* em. : *parivajñitaṃ* Ms

[221] matā em. (*'dod* T) : matī Ms

[222] *durjayānāṃ* em. : *durjaṣānā* Ms

[223] *kleśānāṃ* em. : *kleṣānā* Ms

[224] *sudurjayā* (*sbyaṅ dkar 'dod* T) em. : *sudurjaṣā* Ms ◦

[225] *saṅgrahaḥ* em. : *saṅgrahaṃ* Ms

[226] °*sampadām* em. : °*sampadā* Ms

[227] °*gambhīrā* em. (*zab pa* CGNP : *zad pa* D, 甚深 Ch1) : °*gambhītyā* Ms

krīḍate raśmijālena
cakravyūhaiḥ[228] samantataḥ[229] |
trilokāt[230] tīrṇapaṅkaughair[231]
dūraṅgamā iti smṛtā || <74> [84]

buddhaiḥ san(5a4)dhriyamāṇo[232] 'sau
praviṣṭo[233] jñānasāgare |
anābhogavaśiprāptaḥ
akampyā mārakiṅkaraiḥ || <75> [85]

pratisaṃvitsu sarvāsu[234]
sa yogī pāramīgataḥ |
dharmadeśena sāṅkathyair[235]
bhūmi(5a5)ḥ[236] sādhumatī smṛtā || <76> [86]

kāyaṃ[237] jñānamayaṃ rāmyam[238]
ākāśam iva nirmalam |
sandhārayati buddhānāṃ[239]
dharmameghā[240] samantataḥ || <77> [87]

āśrayaḥ[241] sarvadharmāṇāṃ[242]

---

228 帝釋 = **śakra*° Ch1 for *cakra*°

229 *samantataḥ* em. : *samantata* Ms

230 *trilokāt* (*'khor ba ... de la* T) em. : *strīr l{..}(o ?)kāt* Ms ◦ 欲 Ch1 = **rāgāt* for *lokāt*

231 *tīrṇa*° (*brgal ba* T, 超越 Ch1) em. : *tāra*° Ms ◦ 暴流 Ch1 for °*paṅkaughair*

232 *sandhriyamāṇo* em. (*ṅes 'di bzuṅ* T, 一切(佛)加持 Ch1) : *satvāyamāṇo* Ms

233 *praviṣṭo* em. : *praviṣṭā* Ms

234 *sarvāsu* em. (*kun la* T, 諸 Ch1) : *bharvāsu* Ms

235 *sāṅkathyair* em. : *sāṃkathyai* Ms

236 *bhūmiḥ* em. : *bhūmim* Ms

237 *kāyaṃ* em. : *kāya* Ms

238 *'di yi* T = **tasya* for *rāmyam*

239 *buddhānāṃ* em. : *buddhānā* Ms

240 *dharmameghā* em. : *dharmmameghāḥ* Ms

241 *āśrayaḥ* em. (*āśrayasya* 78c, *gnas* T, 所依 Ch1) : *āśravaḥ* Ms

242 *saṅs rgyas rnams* T, 佛 Ch1 = **buddha*° for *sarva*° ◦ °*dharmāṇāṃ* em. : °*dharmmānā* Ms

caryāphalaparigrahaḥ |
(5b1) āśrayasya parāvṛttir[243]
dharmakāyo 'bhidhīyate[244] || <78> [88]

acintyo vāsanād muktaś[245]
cintyaḥ saṃsāravāsanaḥ[246] |
tvam acintyo 'si sarveṣāṃ[247]
kas tvā[248] vijñātum arhati[249] || <79> [89]

sarvavāgviṣayā(5b2)tītaṃ
sarvendriyam agocaram |
manovijñānagamyo 'si
yo 'si yo 'si[250] namo 'stu te[251] || <80> [90]

krameṇa[252] samudānītā[253]
buddhaputrā[254] mahāyaśāḥ[255] |
dharmameghena jñānena
śūnyaṃ[256] paśyanti dharma(5b3)tām || <81> [91]

yadā prakṣālitaṃ cittam
uttīrṇaṃ[257] bhavasāgarāt[258] |

---

243 *parāvṛttir* em. : *parāvṛtti* Ms

244 *'bhidhīyate* em. (*brjod pa yin* T, 名 Ch1) : *bidhīyate* Ms

245 *vāsanād muktaś* : *vāsanā muktasa* Ms

246 及離流轉習 Ch1 = * *muktaḥ saṃsāravāsanair* for *cintyaḥ saṃsāravāsanaḥ*

247 om. Ch1 for *sarveṣāṃ*

248 *tvā* em. (*khyod ni* T) : *tva* Ms

249 *arhati* em.: *arhasi* Ms

250 *ruṅ la* T = **yogyo* for *yo si*

251 *phyag 'tshal bstod* T = **namo stute* for *namo 'stu te*

252 *krameṇa* em. : *kramena* Ms

253 *samudānītā* em. (*'jug pa'i lugs ñid* T, 積集 Ch1) : *samudrānītā* Ms

254 °*putrā* em. : °*putrāḥ* Ms

255 *mahāyaśāḥ* em. : *mahāyaśā* Ms ◦ *mahāyaśāḥ* for *mahāyaśasaḥ* (*saṅs rgyas sras po grags chen rnams* T), m.c.

256 微細 Ch1 = **sūkṣmaṃ* for *śūnyaṃ*

257 *uttīrṇaṃ* em. : *uttīrṇṇa* Ms

258 *bhavasāgarāt* (生死海 Ch1) : *bhavasāgarān* Ms ◦ *'khor ba'i gzeb las* = **saṃsārapañcarāt* T for *bhavasāgarāt*

mahāpadmamayaṃ tasya
āsanaṃ sampratiṣṭhati || <82> [92]

anekaratnapattrābhaṃ
lakṣaṇojjvalakalpikam[259] |
anekaiḥ padma(5b4)koṭībhiḥ
samantāt parivāritam || <83> [93]

daśabhiś ca balair bālas[260]
tiṣṭhate bālacandravat[261] |
kleśair malinasattvānāṃ[262]
na paśyati tathāgatam[263] || <84> [51]

yadā pretāḥ samantāt[264] tu
śuṣkaṃ[265] paśyanti (5b5) sāgaram[266] |
tathaivājñānadagdhānāṃ[267]
buddho[268] nāstīti kalpanā || <85> [52]

sattvānām[269] alpapuṇyānāṃ[270]
bhagavān kiṃ kariṣyati[271] |
jātya[272]xx⏑—x

---

259 *lakṣaṇojjvalakalpikam* em. : *lakṣaṇaujvalakalpikāṃ* Ms ∘ *'dod par bya ba'i ze'u 'bru can* T, 寶光明為臺 Ch1 for *lakṣaṇojjvalakalpikam*

260 *bālas* em. : *bāla* Ms ∘ *byis pa rnams* = **bālās* T for *bālas*, 彼彼人現化 Ch1 for *daśabhiś ca balair bālas*

261 如水月 Ch1 = **jalacandravat* for *bālacandravat*

262 °*sattvānāṃ* em. : °*sattānaṃ* Ms ∘ *sems can gyis* T, 攪擾心 Ch1 for *malinasattvānāṃ*

263 *tathāgatam* em. : *tathāgataḥ* Ms

264 *samantāt* em. : *samantā* Ms ∘ om. T for *samantāt*

265 *śuṣkaṃ* em. : *śuṣkāṃ* Ms

266 *sāgaram* em. : *sāgaraḥ* Ms

267 °*dagdhānāṃ* em. : °*dagdhānā* Ms ∘ *mi śes pas bsgribs pas* T = **ajñānāvṛtānām*, 少福者 Ch1 = **alpapuṇyānām* for *ajñānadagdhānāṃ*

268 *saṅs rgyas rnams* T for *buddho*

269 *sattvānām* em. : *satvānātm* Ms ∘ *dman pa* T for *sattvānām*

270 *alpapuṇyānāṃ* em. : *aṃlpapuṇyānā* Ms

271 *kiṃ kariṣyati* em. : *kiṅ kariṣyantiḥ* Ms

272 Possibly continuing with *ndhasya yathā haste* (*ji ltar dmus loṅ lag pa ru* T, 如於生盲手 Ch1).

xxxx⏑–⏑x || <86> [53]

Critical Edition of Tibetan Text

(C72a7)(N70a3)(P73a7) chos kyi dbyiṅs bstod pa || ||[1]
(D63b5)(G90b1) rgya gar skad du | dharma dhātu (N70a4) stava[2] | bod skad du | chos kyi dbyiṅs su bstod pa | 'phags pa [3]'jam dpal (C72b1) gźon nur gyur pa la phyag 'tshal (D63b6) lo ||

gaṅ źig kun tu ma śes (P73a8) na ||
srid pa gsum du rnam 'khor ba ||
sems cen kun la ṅes gnas (G90b2) pa[4]'i ||
chos kyi dbyiṅs (N70a5) la phyag 'tshal lo[5] || [1]

gaṅ źig 'khor ba'i rgyur gyur pa ||
de ñid sbyaṅ ba byas pa las ||
dag pa de ñid (C72b2) mya ṅan 'das ||
(P73b1) chos kyi sku yaṅ de ñid do || [2]

(D63b6) ji ltar 'o ma daṅ 'dres pas ||
mar gyi sñiṅ po mi snaṅ ba ||
de bźin ñon moṅs daṅ (G90b3, N70a6) 'dres pas ||
chos kyi dbyiṅs kyaṅ mi mthoṅ ṅo || [3]

(D63b7) ji ltar 'o ma rnams sbyaṅs pas ||
mar gyi (P73b2) sñiṅ po dri med 'gyur ||
de bźin ñon moṅs rnams sbyaṅ (C72b3) pas ||
chos dbyiṅs śin tu dri med 'gyur || [4]

(D64a1) ji ltar mar me bum naṅ gnas ||
(N70a7) cuṅ źig snaṅ (G90b4) bar mi 'gyur ba ||
de bźin ñon moṅs bum naṅ[6] gnas ||
(P73b3) chos kyi dbyiṅs kyaṅ mi mthoṅ ṅo || [5]

phyogs ni gaṅ daṅ gaṅ dag nas ||
bum pa bu ga gtoṅ gyur pa ||

---

[1] om. DG.

[2] *dharma dhātu stabaṃ* D; *dharma dha tu stotra* CGNP.

[3] om. CGNP.

[4] *ba* G.

[5] *'tshal 'dud* GN.

[6] *na* C.

de daṅ (C72b4) de yi phyogs ñid nas ||
'od kyi raṅ bźin 'byuṅ (D64a2) bar (N70b1) 'gyur || [6]

gaṅ tshe tiṅ 'dzin rdo rje (G90b5) yis ||
(P73b4) bum ba de ni bcag gyur pa ||
de tshe de ni nam[7] mkha' yi ||
mthar thug par du snaṅ bar byed || [7]

chos kyi dbyiṅs ni skye ma yin ||
nam yaṅ 'gag par 'gyur ba med ||
dus rnams (C72b5) kun tu ñon moṅs (N70b2) med ||
thog ma bar mthar[8] dri ma bral || (D64a3, P73b5) [8]

ji ltar (G90b6) rin chen bai ḍū rya ||
dus rnams kun tu 'od gsal yaṅ ||
rdo yi naṅ na gnas gyur na ||
de[9] yi 'od ni gsal ma yin |||| [9]

de bźin ñon moṅs kyis bsgribs pa'i ||
chos dbyiṅs śin tu dri med pa'aṅ ||
(C72b6, N70b3, P73b6) 'khor bar 'od ni gsal ma yin ||
mya ṅan 'das (G91a1) na 'od gsal (D64a4) 'gyur || [10]

khams yod na ni las byas pas ||
sa le sbram dag mthoṅ bar 'gyur ||
khams med par ni las byas na'aṅ[10] ||
ñon moṅs 'ba' źig (P73b7) skyed[11] bar zad || [11]

ji ltar (N70b4) sbun pas g.yogs gyur (C72b7) pas ||
(G91a2) so ba 'bras bu mi 'dod ltar ||
de bźin ñon moṅs kyis g.yogs (D64a5) pas ||
de ni[12] saṅs rgyas źes mi brtag || [12]

ji ltar sbun pa las grol na ||

---

[7] *na* GN.

[8] *mtha'* CNP; *mtha'i* G.

[9] *di* P.

[10] *na* D.

[11] *bskyed* D.

[12] *nas* P.

(P73b8) bras ñid snaṅ bar 'gyur ba ltar ||
de bźin ñon moṅs las (N70b5) grol na ||
chos kyi sku ñid rab tu (C73a1) gsal || [13]

(G91a3) chu śiṅ sñiṅ po med do źes ||
'jig rten na ni dper byed kyaṅ ||
de yi 'bras bu sñiṅ po (D64a6) ñid ||
(P74a1) mṅar po za bar byed pa ltar || [14]

sñiṅ po med pa'i 'khor ba las ||
ñon moṅs gzeb[13] daṅ bral gyur na ||
de yi 'bras (C73a2, N70b6) bu saṅs rgyas[14] ñid ||
lus can kun (G91a4) gyi bdud rtsir gyur || [15]

de bźin sa bon (P74a2) thams cad las ||
rgyu daṅ 'dra[15] ba'i 'bras bu 'byuṅ ||
sa bon med (D64a7) par 'bras yod par ||
śes ldan gaṅ gis bsgrub par nus || [16]

sa bon gyur pa khams de ñid ||
(N70b7) chos rnams (C73a3) kun gyi rten du 'dod ||
rim (G91a5, P74a3) gyis sbyaṅs par gyur ba las ||
saṅs rgyas go 'phaṅ thob par 'gyur || [17]

dri med ñi ma zla ba yaṅ ||
sprin daṅ khug rna du ba[16] daṅ ||
sgra (D64b1) gcan gdoṅ daṅ rdul la sogs ||
sgrib pa lṅa yis bsgribs par 'gyur || [18]

(N71a1, P74a4) de bźin 'od (C73a4) gsal ba yi sems ||
'dod (G91a6) daṅ gnod sems le lo daṅ ||
rgod pa daṅ ni the tshom ste ||
sgrib pa lṅa yis bsgribs par gyur || [19]

ji ltar me yis dag pa'i gos ||
sna tshogs (D64b2) dri mas dri ma can ||

---

13 *gzib* P.

14 *sñiṅ po* CGNP.

15 *'bra* P.

16 *du ba khug rna* CGNP.

(P74a5) ji ltar me yi (N71a2) naṅ bcug na ||
dri ma tshig 'gyur gos (C73a5) min ltar || [20]

de bźin 'od (G91b1) gsal ba yi sems ||
'dod chags la sogs dri ma can ||
ye śes me yis dri ma[17] bsreg ||
de ñid 'od gsal ma yin no[18] || [21]

stoṅ pa ñid ni ston pa'i mdo ||
(P74a6) rgyal bas (D64b3) ji sñed (N71a3) gsuṅs pa gaṅ ||
de dag kun gyis ñon moṅs ldog ||
(C73a6) khams de ñams par (G91b2) byed ma yin || [22]

sa yi naṅ na gnas pa'i[19] chu ||
dri ma med par gnas pa ltar ||
ñon moṅs naṅ na ye śes kyaṅ ||
(P74a7) de bźin dri ma med par gnas || [23]

chos (N71a4) dbyiṅs gaṅ phyir bdag ma (D64b4) yin ||
bud med ma yin skyes pa min ||
gzuṅ ba (C73a7) kun las rnam grol (G91b3) ba ||
ji ltar bdag ces brtag par bya || [24]

chags pa med pa'i chos kun la ||
(P74a8) bud med skyes pa dmigs ma yin ||
'dod chags kyis (N71a5) ldoṅs[20] gdul bya'i phyir ||
bud med skyes pa śes rab bstan || [25]

(D64b5) mi rtag sdug bsṅal (C73b1) stoṅ pa źes ||
bya ba gsum (G91b4) pos sems sbyoṅ byed ||
mchog tu sems (P74b1) ni sbyoṅ byed pa'i ||
chos ni raṅ bźin med pa yin || [26]

ji ltar sbrum ma'i lto na (N71a6) bu ||
yod kyaṅ mthoṅ ba ma yin pa ||
de bźin ñon moṅs kyis g.yogs pa'i ||

---

[17] *ñon moṅs* D.

[18] *yi no* G.

[19] *dkyil na yod pa'i* D.

[20] *gduṅs* CGNP.

chos kyi (C73b2) dbyiṅs kyaṅ (D64b6) mthoṅ ma yin || [27]

(G91b5) bdag daṅ (P74b2) bdag gi rnam rtog daṅ ||
miṅ gi 'du śes rgyu mtshan gyis ||
rnam rtog bźi po 'byuṅ ba yaṅ ||
'byuṅ (N71a7) daṅ 'byuṅ las gyur pas so || [28]

saṅs rgyas rnams kyi smon lam[21] yaṅ ||
snaṅ ba med ciṅ(C73b3) mtshan (P74b3) ñid med ||
so sor[22] raṅ rig sbyor (G91b6) ldan ñid ||
(D64b7) saṅs rgyas rtag pa'i chos ñid can || [29]

ji ltar ri boṅ mgo bo'i rwa ||
brtags[23] pa ñid de med pa ltar ||
(N71b1) de bźin chos rnams thams cad kyaṅ ||
brtags[24] (P74b4) pa ñid de yod ma yin || [30]

phra rab rdul gyi ṅo bo yis ||
(C73b4) glaṅ gi rwa yaṅ yod[25] ma yin || (G92a1)
ji ltar sṅon bźin phyis de bźin ||
de (D65a1) la ci źig brtag par bya || [31]

brten nas 'byuṅ bar 'gyur ba daṅ ||
(N71b2) brten nas 'gag (P74b5) par 'gyur bas na ||
gcig kyaṅ yod pa ma yin no ||
byis pas[26] ji ltar rtogs par byed || [32]

ri boṅ (G92a2) ba laṅ rwa (C73b5) yi dpes ||
xxxxxxx ||
ji ltar bde gśegs chos rnams ñid ||
dbu ma ñid du sgrub (D65a2) par byed || [33]

ji ltar (P74b6) ñi zla skar (N71b3) ma'i gzugs ||
dag pa'i snod kyi chu naṅ du ||

---

21 *lan* G.

22 *so* G.

23 *btags* CGNP.

24 *btags* CGNP.

25 *dmigs* D.

26 *pa* D.

gzugs brñan mthoṅ bar 'gyur ba ltar ||
mtshan ñid rdzogs pa'aṅ de daṅ (G92a3) 'dra || [34]

thog ma bar daṅ mthar (C73b6) dge ba ||
bslu ba med ciṅ brtan (P74b7) pa yi ||
gaṅ źig de ltar bdag med pa'aṅ [27] ||
ji (N71b4) ltar bdag (D65a3) daṅ bdag gir brtag || [35]

ji ltar sos ka'i[28] dus su chu ||
dro bo[29] źes ni brjod par byed ||
de ñid graṅ ba'i dus su ni ||
graṅ ṅo (G92a4) źes ni brjod pa yin || [36]

(P74b8) ñon moṅs dra bas (C73b7) g.yogs pa ni[30] ||
sems can źes ni brjod par bya ||
de ñid (N71b5) ñon moṅs bral gyur na ||
saṅs rgyas źes ni brjod par (D65a4) bya || [37]

mig daṅ gzugs la brten nas ni ||
dri ma med pa'i snaṅ pa 'byuṅ ||
(P75a1) skye (G92a5) med 'gag pa med ñid las ||
chos kyi dbyiṅs ni rab (C74a1) tu śes || [38]

sgra daṅ rna ba la brten nas ||
(N71b6) rnam par dag pa'i śes pa gsum ||
mtshan ñid med pa chos kyi dbyiṅs ||
rtog daṅ (P75a2) bcas pas (D65a5) thos par 'gyur || [39]

sna daṅ dri la brten nas snom ||
(G92a6) de ni[31] gzugs su med pa'i dpe[32] ||
(C74a2) de bźin sna yi rnam śes kyis ||
chos kyi dbyiṅs (N71b7) la rtog par byed || [40]

lce yi raṅ bźin stoṅ pa ñid ||

---

[27] *la* CGNP.

[28] *so ga'i* D.

[29] *'o* D, *bos* CP.

[30] *na* CGNP.

[31] om. C.

[32] *dpes* D.

ro yi khams (P75a3) kyaṅ dben pa ste ||
chos kyi dbyiṅs kyi ṅo bo yin[33] ||
rnam par śes (D65a6) pa gnas med pa || [41]

dag (G92b1) pa'i lus kyi ṅo bo daṅ ||
reg (C74a3) bya'i rkyen gyi mtshan ñid dag ||
rkyen dag las ni (N72a1) grol gyur pa ||
chos kyi dbyiṅs źes (P75a4) brjod par bya || [42]

yid gtsor gyur pa'i chos rnams la ||
rtog daṅ brtag pa rnam spaṅs nas ||
chos rnams raṅ bźin med pa (G92b2) ñid ||
(D65a7) chos kyi dbyiṅs su (C74a4) bsgom par bya || [43]

mthoṅ (N72a2) daṅ thos daṅ bsnams[34] pa daṅ ||
(P75a5) myaṅs daṅ reg par gyur pa daṅ ||
chos rnams de ltar rnal 'byor pas ||
śes nas mtshan ñid rdzogs pa yin || [44]

mig daṅ rna ba sna dag daṅ ||
lce daṅ lus (G92b3) daṅ de bźin yid ||
skye (C74a5) mched (D65b1) drug po rnam (N72a3) dag (P75a6) pa ||
'di ñid de ñid mtshan ñid do || [45]

sems ñid rnam pa gñis su mthoṅ[35] ||
ji ltar 'jig rten 'jig rten 'das ||
bdag du 'dzin las 'khor ba ste ||
so sor rig na de ñid do || [46]

'dod chags zad pas (G92b4) mya ṅan (P75a7) 'das ||
źe (C74a6) sdaṅ gti mug zad pa (N72a4) daṅ ||
de dag (D65b2) 'gags pas saṅs rgyas ñid ||
lus can kun gyi skyabs ñid do || [47]

śes daṅ mi śes pa dag las ||
lus 'di ñid la[36] thams cad de ||

---

33 *yis* CGNP.

34 *bsnoms* C.

35 *mtho* CGNP.

raṅ gi rnam par (P75a8) rtog pas bciṅs ||
bdag ñid (G92b5) śes nas[37] grol bar 'gyur || [48]

(C74a7) byaṅ chub riṅ min (N72a5) ñe ba'aṅ[38] min ||
'gro min 'oṅ ba'aṅ[39] ma yin źiṅ ||
(D65b3) ñon moṅs gzeb gyur 'di ñid la ||
mthoṅ ba daṅ ni ma mthoṅ yin || [49]

(P75b1) śes rab mar me la gnas nas ||
mchog tu źi bar gyur pa yis ||
(G92b6) bdag la brtags pas[40] gnas bya źes ||
(C74b1) mdo (N72a6) sde'i tshogs las gsuṅs pa lags || [50]

stobs bcu'i stobs kyis byis[41] pa rnams ||
(D65b4, P75b2) byin brlabs[42] zla ba tshes pa bźin ||
ñon moṅs can gyi sems can gyis ||
de bźin gśegs pa mi mthoṅ ṅo || [51]

(G93a1) ji ltar yi dwags[43] rnams kyis ni ||
rgya (N72a7) mtsho bskams[44] (C74b2) par mthoṅ ba ltar ||
de bźin (P75b3) mi śes pas bsgribs pas ||
saṅs rgyas rnams ni med par brtags || [52]

dman (D65b5) pa[45] bsod nams dman pa la ||
bcom ldan 'das kyis (G93a2) ci bgyir mchis ||
ji ltar dmus loṅ lag pa ru ||
(N72b1, P75b4) rin chen mchog ni bźag pa 'dra || [53]

(C74b3) sems can bsod nams byas rnams la ||

---

36 *las* CGNP.

37 *na* D.

38 *ba* D.

39 *ba* D.

40 *rtag par* CGNP.

41 *byin* C; *byas* P.

42 *rlabs* D.

43 *dags* D.

44 *skams* D.

45 *daṅ* D.

'od kyis gsal źiṅ dpal ldan pa'i ||
sum cu rtsa gñis mtshan 'bar ba ||
(D65b6) saṅs rgyas de yi mdun na (G93a3) gnas || [54]

mgon (P75b5) po de yi gzugs kyi skus[46] ||
bskal pa maṅ por (N72b2) bźugs nas kyaṅ [47] ||
gdul bya rnams ni 'dul (C74b4) ba'i phyir ||
dbyiṅs ñid tha dad gyur pa lags || [55]

sems kyi yul ni des rtogs nas ||
der ni śes pa 'jug (P75b6) par 'gyur ||
so sor raṅ (D65b7, G93a4) rig rnam[48] dag na ||
sa rnams de yi bdag ñid gnas || [56]

dbaṅ phyug (N72b3) chen po'i gnas mchog daṅ ||
'og min ñid de (C74b5) rnam mdzes pa ||
śes pa gsum po gcig ñid du ||
(P75b7) 'dres par gyur la bdag smra 'o || [57]

byis pa'i naṅ na yoṅs [49] mkhyen daṅ ||
(G93a5) 'phags pa'i naṅ na sna tshogs ñid ||
(D66a1) dbaṅ phyug chen po tshe dpag med ||
bskal (N72b4) pa'i[50] tshe yi rgyu gaṅ yin || [58]

(C74b6) phyi rol sems can (P75b8) khams [51] kyi yaṅ ||
dpag tu med pa'i bskal par ni ||
tshe[52] yaṅ gaṅ gis bsruṅs gyur ciṅ ||
srog chags rnams[53] gyi srog (G93a6) gnas pa'i || [59]

rgyu yaṅ mi zad pa de ñid ||
(D66a2) gaṅ gis 'bras bu mi zad (N72b5) gaṅ ||

---

46 *sku* CGNP.

47 *ni* CGNP.

48 *rnams* P.

49 *kun* CGNP.

50 *pa* CGNP.

51 *mkhas* CGNP.

52 *che* P.

53 *kun* CGNP.

(P76a1) snaṅ ba med pa'i bye brag gis ||
(C74b7) śes rab don du rab tu 'jug || [60]

byaṅ chub riṅ bar mi bsam źiṅ ||
ñe bar yaṅ ni bsam mi bya ||
yul drug snaṅ ba med par ni ||
(G93b1) yaṅ dag ji bźin (P76a2) rig gyur pa'o || [61]

ji ltar 'o ma daṅ 'dras (N72b6) chu ||
snod gcig la[54] ni (D66a3) gnas pa las ||
ṅaṅ pas[55] 'o ma 'thuṅ (C75a1) byed ciṅ ||
chu ni ma yin de bźin gnas || [62]

de bźin ñon moṅs kyis g.yogs nas ||
ye śes (P76a3) lus 'dir (G93b2) gcig nas kyaṅ ||
rnal 'byor pa yis ye śes len ||
(N72b7) mi śes pa ni 'dor bar byed || [63]

bdag daṅ bdag (C75a2) gi źes 'dzin pas ||
(D66a4) ji srid phyi rol rnam brtags pa[56] ||
bdag med rnam pa gñis (P76a4) mthoṅ na[57] ||
srid pa'i sa bon 'gag par (G93b3) 'gyur || [64]

gaṅ phyir saṅs rgyas mya ṅan 'das ||
gtsaṅ ba (N73a1) rtag pa dge ba'i gźi ||
gaṅ[58] phyir gñis ni byis pas (C75a3) brtags[59] ||
de yi gñis med rnal (P76a5) 'byor gnas || [65]

dka' spyod sna (D66a5) tshogs sbyin pa daṅ ||
tshul khrims sems can don sdud daṅ ||
sems (G93b4) can phan byed bzod pa ste ||
(N73a2) gsum po 'di yis[60] khams rgyas 'gyur || [66]

---

[54] *na* D.

[55] *pa* D.

[56] *btags pa* CGNP.

[57] *nas* CGNP.

[58] *dag* CGNP.

[59] *btags* GNP; *gtags* C.

[60] *'dis ni* D.

chos rnams (P76a6) kun la brtson (C75a4) 'grus daṅ ||
bsam gtan la sems 'jug pa daṅ ||
rtag tu śes rab brtan [61] pa ste ||
'di yaṅ byaṅ chub (D66a6) rgyas byed yin || [67]

thabs daṅ (G93b5) bcas pa'i śes rab daṅ ||
(N73a3) smon lam (P76a7) rnam par sbyaṅs pa daṅ ||
stobs la ṅes gnas[62] ye śes te ||
(C75a5) khams rgyas byed pa'i chos bźi po[63] || [68]

byaṅ chub sems phyag mi bya źes ||
smra ba ṅan[64] pa smra ba ste ||
byaṅ chub sems dpa' ma byuṅ bar ||
(P75a8) chos (G93b6) kyi sku (D66a7) ni 'byuṅ (N73a4) ma yin || [69]

bur śiṅ sa bon la sdaṅ gaṅ ||
kha ra spyad par 'dod pa des[65] ||
(C75a6) bur śiṅ sa bon med par ni ||
kha ra 'byuṅ bar 'gyur ma yin || [70]

bur śiṅ sa bon gaṅ bsruṅs nas ||
(P76b1) ñe bar gnas śiṅ bsgrubs pa las ||
bu ram kha ra (G94a1, N73a5) hwags rnams ni ||
de las 'byuṅ (D66b1) bar 'gyur ba ltar || [71]

byaṅ chub sems ni (C75a7) rab bsruṅs nas ||
ñe bar gnas śiṅ bsgrubs ba las ||
dgra bcom rkyen (P76b2) rtogs saṅs rgyas rnams ||
de las skye źiṅ 'byuṅ bar 'gyur || [72]

ji ltar sā (G94a2) lu'i (N73a6) sa bon sogs ||
źiṅ pas bsruṅ[66] bar byed pa ltar ||

---

[61] *bstan* D.

[62] *des nas* D.

[63] *'o* D.

[64] *na* P.

[65] *de* P.

[66] *sruṅs* C.

de bźin theg (C75b1) mchog mos rnams (D66b2) la'aṅ[67]||
'dren pa rnams kyis bsruṅ bar[68] (P76b3) mdzad || [73]

ji ltar mar ṅo'i bcu bźi la ||
zla ba cuṅ zad[69] mthoṅ ba ltar ||
de bźin theg mchog mos (N73a7) rnams la 'aṅ ||
saṅs (G94a3) rgyas sku ni cuṅ zad mthoṅ[70] || [74]

ji ltar tshes pa'i zla ba la ||
skad cig (C75b2) skad cig (P76b4) rgyas par mthoṅ ||
de bźin sa la źugs (D66b3) rnams kyaṅ ||
rim gyis rim gyis rgyas[71] par mthoṅ || [75]

ji ltar yar ṅo'i bco lṅa la ||
(N73b1) zla ba rdzogs par 'gyur ba ltar ||
de bźin sa (G94a4) yi mthar thug na ||
chos kyi sku (P76b5) yaṅ rdzogs śiṅ gsal || [76]

(C75b3) saṅs rgyas chos daṅ dge 'dun la ||
rtag tu mos pa brtan po yis ||
sems (D66b4) de yaṅ dag bskyed byas nas ||
phyir mi ldog par[72] yaṅ yaṅ (N73b2) 'byuṅ || [77]

nag po'i gźi ni yoṅs (P76b6) spaṅs nas ||
dkar (G94a5) po'i gźi ni rab bzuṅ bas ||
de tshe de ni ṅes rtogs pa ||
(C75b4) dga' ba źes ni mṅon par brjod || [78]

'dod chags la sogs sna tshogs pa'i ||
dri mas rtag tu dri ma (D66b5) can ||
dri ma med par[73] (P76b7) gaṅ dag pa ||
(N73b3) dri ma med ces brjod pa yin || [79]

---

67 *la* CGNP.

68 *ba* CGNP.

69 *źig* CGNP.

70 *snaṅ* CGNP.

71 *'phel* D.

72 *pa* CGNP.

73 *pas* CGNP.

ñon moṅs dra ba rab (G94a6) 'gags nas ||
dri med śes[74] rab rab gsal bas ||
tshad med pa (C75b5) yi mun pa dag ||
sel bar byed pas 'od byed pa'o || [80]

rtag tu dag (P76b8) pa'i 'od kyis gsal ||
'du 'dzi rnam par spaṅs pa yi ||
(D66b6, N73b4) ye śes 'od kyis rab bskor bas ||
sa de 'od 'phro can du (G94b1) 'dod || [81]

rig daṅ sgyu rtsal bzo gnas kun ||
bsam gtan rnam pa sna (C75b6) tshogs (P77a1) ñid ||
ñon moṅs śin tu sbyaṅ dka' las ||
rnam par rgyal bas sbyaṅ dkar 'dod || [82]

byaṅ chub (N73b5) rnam pa gsum po daṅ ||
phun sum tshogs (D66b7) kun bsdu ba daṅ ||
skye daṅ (G94b2) 'jig pa (P77a2) zab[75] pa la ||
sa de mṅon du gyur par 'dod || [83]

'khor lo'i bkod pas[76] (C75b7) rnam kun tu[77] ||
'od kyi dra bas rtse ba daṅ ||
'khor ba'i mtsho yi 'dam brgal bas ||
(N73b6) de la riṅ du soṅ źes bya || [84]

saṅs rgyas kyis (P77a3) ṅes 'di bzuṅ źiṅ ||
ye śes rgya (D67a1, G94b3) mtshor źugs pa daṅ ||
'bad med lhun gyis grub gyur pa[78] ||
bdud kyi 'khor gyis mi g.yo (C76a1) ba'o[79] || [85]

so so yaṅ dag rig kun la ||
chos ston pa yi 'bel (N73b7) pa'i gtam ||
(P77a4) rnal 'byor pa de mthar son pas ||

---

[74] *śe* C.

[75] *zad* D.

[76] *pa* D.

[77] *du* D.

[78] *pas* CGNP.

[79] *g.yos pa'o* D.

sa de legs pa'i blo gros 'dod || [86]

ye (G94b4) śes (D67a2) raṅ bźin 'di yi sku ||
dri med nam[80] mkha' daṅ mñam pa ||
(C76a2) saṅs rgyas rnams kyi 'dzin pa las ||
chos kyi sprin ni (P77a5) kun tu 'byuṅ || [87]

saṅs (N74a1) rgyas rnams kyi chos kyi gnas ||
spyod pa'i 'bras bu yoṅs 'dzin pas ||
gnas ni yoṅs[81] su gyur pa (G94b5) de ||
chos kyi sku źes brjod pa (D67a3) yin || [88]

bag chags las grol (C76a3) bsam (P77a6) mi khyab ||
'khor ba'i bag chags bsam du (N74a2) yod ||
khyod ni kun tu bsam mi khyab ||
gaṅ gis khyod ni śes par nus || [89]

ṅag gi spyod yul kun las 'das ||
dbaṅ po (G94b6) kun gyi spyod yul min ||
(P77a7) yid gyi śes pas rtogs bya ba ||
gaṅ yaṅ (C76a4, D67a4) ruṅ la phyag 'tshal bstod || [90]

rim gyis (N74a3) 'jug pa'i lugs ñid kyis ||
saṅs rgyas sras po grags chen rnams ||
chos kyi sprin gyi ye śes kyis ||
chos ñid stoṅ (P77a8) pa mthoṅ (G95a1) gyur nas || [91] [82]

gaṅ tshe sems ni rab bkrus (C76a5) pas ||
'khor (N74a4) ba'i gzeb las 'das gyur nas[83] ||
pad ma chen po'i[84] raṅ (D67a5) bźin gyi ||
stan la de ni rab gnas 'gyur || [92]

(P77b1) 'dab ma rin chen du ma'i 'od ||
'dod (G95a2) par bya ba'i ze'u[85] 'bru can ||

---

[80] *na* CGNP.

[81] *yoṅ* GN.

[82] Even one stanza more: *pad ma chen po'i raṅ bźin gyis* | CGNP.

[83] *gyur* GP.

[84] *po* CN.

[85] *ze* D.

pad ma bye ba du ma yis ||
rnam pa kun tu yoṅs su bskor || [93]

(C76a6) stobs (N74a5) bcu po yis yoṅs su gaṅ ||
mi 'jigs pa yis gaṅ[86] dag ṅoms ||
(P77b2) bsam mi khyab pa'i saṅs rgyas (D67a6) chos ||
spros med rnams las ñams mi mṅa' || [94]

(G95a3) legs par spyod pa'i las kun gyis ||
bsod nams ye śes rab bsags (N74a6) pa'i ||
zla (C76a7) ba ña la skar ma yis ||
(P77b3) 'khor du rnam pa kun gyis bskor || [95]

saṅs rgyas phyag gi[87] ñi ma der ||
dri med rin chen 'bar gyur des[88] ||
sras kyi thu (D67a7) bo dbaṅ bskur bas ||
dbaṅ (G95a4) bskur ba ni kun tu stsol || [96]

rnal 'byor chen po der (N74a7) gnas (P77b4) nas ||
rmoṅs pas (C76b1) dman pa'i 'jig rten rnams ||
sdug bsṅal gyis g.yeṅs 'jigs pa la ||
lha yi spyan gyis gzigs gyur nas || [97]

de yi sku la 'od zer rnams ||
'bad pa med par[89] 'byuṅ (D67b1) 'gyur (G95a5) te ||
(P77b5) rmoṅs pa'i (N74b1) mun par źugs de yi ||
sgo rnams 'byed par mdzad pa yin || [98]

lhag (C76b2) bcas mya ṅan 'das pa rnams ||
lhag med mya ṅan 'das par 'dod ||
'dir ni mya ṅan 'das pa ñid ||
dri ma med par sems (P77b6) gyur pa'o || [99]

sems can kun gyi dṅos med (G95a6, N74b2) pa'i ||
ṅo bo de (D67b2) yaṅ de'i spyod yul ||
de mthoṅ byaṅ chub sems dbaṅ po [90] ||

---

[86] *yaṅ* CGNP.

[87] *chagi* N.

[88] *te* D

[89] *ra* C.

śin tu dri med chos (C76b3) kyi sku || [100]

dri ma med pa'i chos sku la ||
ye śes rgya mtsho gnas (P77b7) gyur nas ||
sna tshogs nor bu ji bźin du ||
de las[91] sems can don rnams (N74b3) mdzad || [101]

chos kyi dbyiṅs su (G95b1) bstod pa slob dpon 'phags pa[92] klu sgrub kyis (D67b3) mdzad pa rdzogs so || (P77b8) rgya gar gyi[93] mkhan (C76b4) po kṛṣṇa paṇḍita daṅ | lo tsā ba[94] tshul khrims rgyal bas bsgyur ba'o ||

---

[90] *dpa'o* CGNP.

[91] *de das* CGNP

[92] *chen po* D.

[93] om. C.

[94] *lo tsā ba dge sloṅ* GNP.

Critical Edition of Chinese Texts

Taishō 413 百千頌大集經地藏菩薩請問法身讚

開府儀同三司特進試鴻臚卿肅國公食邑三千戶賜紫贈司空謚大鑒正號大廣智大興善寺三藏沙門不空奉詔譯

歸命禮法身　住於諸有情
彼由不遍知　輪迴於三有{1}<1>
其性即生死　淨時亦復然
清淨是涅槃　亦即是法身{2}<2>
譬如乳相雜　醍醐不可得
如煩惱相雜　法界不可見{3}<3>
譬如淨乳已　酥精妙無垢
如淨其煩惱　法界極清淨{4}<4>
如燈在其瓶　光耀無所有
如在煩惱瓶　法界不照耀[1]{5}<5>
彼彼令一邊　其瓶若得穴
由彼彼一邊　光明而外出{6}<6>
以三摩地杵　破壞煩惱瓶
遍滿於虛空　普遍光照耀[2]{7}<7>
法界亦不生　亦不曾[3]壞滅
一切時不染　初中常無垢{8}<8>
譬如吠瑠璃　常時極光明
石藏以覆蔽　彼光不照耀[4]{9}<9>

---

[1] 耀：曜 CAT
[2] 耀：曜 CAT
[3] 曾：增 CAT
[4] 耀：曜 CAT

如是煩惱覆　法界妙清淨
不照於生死　於涅槃光明{10}<10>
有性若有功　則見於真金
無性若有功　困而無所獲{11}<11>
如糠覆其上　不名為粳米
煩惱覆其上　亦不名為佛{12}<12>
若得離於糠　顯現於粳米
遠離於煩惱　法身得顯現{13}<13>
世間作譬喻　芭蕉無堅實
而有真[5]實果　食味如甘露{14}<14>
如無實生死　流轉煩惱海
其果即佛體　甘露施有施{15}<15>
如是於諸種　相似生其果
無種亦無果　智者必不信{16}<16>
種子則其性　諸法之所依
次第若能淨　獲得成佛位{17}<17>
日月常無垢　以五種覆蔽
雲霧與烟等　羅睺手及塵{18}<18>
如是心光明　覆蔽以五垢
貪愛瞋恚眠　掉舉與疑惑{19}<19>
如火洗其衣　種種垢不淨
若擲於火中　燒垢不燒衣{20}<20>
空類諸契經　所有如來說
一切斷煩惱　不曾壞其性{21}<22>
譬如地下水　常住而清淨
智隱於煩惱　清淨亦復然{22}<23>

[5] 真 (*sārāṇi* Skt., *sñiṅ po ñid* T) : 貞 Taishō

法界亦非我　非女亦非男
遠離一切執　云何分別我{23}<24>
諸法無所著　女男不可得
貪盲調伏故　示現男女相{24}<25>
無常苦空性　心淨慮有三
最勝心淨慮　諸法無自性{25}<26>
如胞胎孕者[6]　有之而不現
如煩惱所覆　法實不可見{26}<27>
分別有四種　所生大造者
分別我我所　名想及境界{27}<28>
一切佛大願　無所有無相
自覺相應故　諸佛常法性{28}<29>
如言兔有角　分別而非有
如是一切法　分別不可得{29}<30>
分析[7]如微塵　分別不可得
如初後亦爾　智云何分別{30}<31>
如是和合生　和合亦滅壞
一法自不生　云何愚分別{31}<32>
兔牛二角喻　此名遍計相
依住於中道　如善逝法性{32}<33>
如月及星宿　現於清水器
影像而顯現　如是圓成相{33}<34>
初中亦為善　常恒不欺誑
彼無五種我　云何我分別{34}<35>
譬如熱時水　故名為熱水
是則共冷時　則名為冷水{35}<36>

---

[6] 者 (*garbhiṇāṃ* Skt., *sbrum ma'i* T) : 子 Taishō

[7] 析 : 折 CAT

覆蔽煩惱網　是則名為心
若離其煩惱　則名為等覺{36}<37>
眼識緣於色　影像極清淨
不生亦不滅　法界如是知[8]{37}<38>
耳識緣於聲　清淨識三種
以自分別聞　法界無形相{38}<39>
鼻依香而嗅　無色亦無形
鼻識是真如　法界應分別{39}<40>
舌界自性空　味界性遠離
無依亦無識　法界自性故{40}<41>
清淨身自性　所觸和合相
遠離於所緣　我說為法界{41}<42>
諸法意為最　離能所分別
法界無自性　法界而分別{42}<43>
能見聞而嗅　是味及所觸
瑜伽法是知　如是圓成相{43}<44>
眼耳及與鼻　舌身及末那
六處皆清淨　如是彼之相{44}<45>
心見有二種　世間出世間
我執為流轉　自覺是真如{45}<46>
無盡是涅槃　若盡貪及癡
覺彼是佛體　有情歸依處{46}<47>
一切於此身　有智及無智
繫縛自分別　由悟得解脫{47}<48>
菩提不遠近　不來亦不去

---

[8] 如是知 (*prajānatha* Skt., *chos kyi dbyiṅs ni rab tu śes* T) : 無形相 Taishō, which should have been a eye-skip to the last *pāda* of next stanza during the working on print plate.

壞滅及顯現　於此煩惱網{48}<49>
說於眾契經　住於自思惟
照以智慧燈　即得最勝寂{49}<50>
菩提不遠想　亦無隣近想
是六境[9]影像　皆由如是知{50}<51>
如水與乳合　同在於一器
鵝飲盡其乳　其水如常在{51}<52>
如是煩惱雜　智在於一器
瑜伽者飲智　棄捨於煩惱{52}<53>
如是我我執　乃至所取執
若見二無我　有種而滅壞{53}<54>
是佛般涅槃　常恒淨無垢
愚夫二分別　無二瑜伽句{54}<55>
種種難行施　以戒攝有情
一切損忍辱　界增此為三{55}<56>
於諸法精進　靜慮心加行
常習於智慧　復得菩提增{56}<57>
方便共為慧　以願皆清淨
以力妙堅智　界增為四種{57}<58>
不應禮菩薩　此為甚惡說
不親於菩薩　不生其法身{58}<59>
憎[10]於甘蔗種　欲食於石蜜
若壞甘蔗種　無由石蜜生{59}<60>
若護甘蔗種　三種而可得
糖半糖石蜜　於中必得生{60}<61>
若護菩提心　三種而可得

---

9 境 (*viṣaya*° Skt., *yul* T) : 種 CAT

10 憎 (*sdaṅ* T) : 增 Taishō

羅漢緣覺佛　於中必得生{61}<62>
如護於稻芽　農夫必當護[11]
如初勝解行　如來必作護{62}<63>
如黑十五日[12]　而見月輪形
如是勝解行　影現佛形相{63}<64>
如是初月輪　刹那刹那增
如是入地者　念念見增益{64}<65>
如白十五日　月輪得圓滿
如是究竟地　法身而得生{65}<66>
勝解彼堅固　常當於佛法
能發如是心　得為不退轉{66}<67>
染依得轉依　得受為淨依
由分得覺悟　名為極喜地{67}<68>
常時於染污　欲等種種[13]垢
無垢得清淨　名為離垢地{68}<69>
滅壞煩惱網　照耀[14]得離垢
無量之暗瞑　離名發光地{69}<70>
清淨常光明　遠離世吉祥
圍遶智慧焰　名為焰慧地{70}<71>
一切明工技　種種靜慮[15]飾
難勝於煩惱　得勝難勝地{71}<72>
於三種菩提　攝受令成就
生滅於甚深　名為現前地{72}<73>

---

[11] 必當護 (*rakṣāṃ kurvanti* Skt., *bsruṅ bar bye pa* T) : 生當護 CAT

[12] 黑十五日 (*kṛṣṇacaturdaśyāṃ* Skt., *mar ṅo'i bcu bźi la*T) : 白十五日 Taishō

[13] 種種 (*vividhair* Skt., *sna tshogs pa* T) : 相種 CAT

[14] 耀 : 曜 CAT

[15] 靜慮 (°*dhyāna*° Skt., *bsam gtan* T) : 淨慮 CAT

遊戲於光網　遍以帝釋嚴
超越欲暴流　名為遠行地{73}<74>
一切佛加持　預入於智海
自在無功用　不動於魔使{74}<75>
於諸無礙解　瑜伽到彼岸
於說法談論　名為善慧地{75}<76>
身以智所成　如虛空無垢
諸佛皆所持　普遍如法雲{76}<77>
佛法之所依　行果皆所持
所依皆得轉　故名為法身{77}<78>
離不思議熏　及離流轉習
汝不思思者[16]　云何而得知{78}<79>
超過諸語境　一切根非境
意識所取者　如所有我禮[17]{79}<80>
次第而積集　佛子大名稱
皆以法雲智　微細見法性{80}<81>
爾時洗濯心　超渡[18]生死海
彼以大蓮花　安立為大座{81}<82>
無量寶葉光　寶光明為臺
無量億蓮花　普遍為眷屬{82}<83>
先以十種力　以無畏四種
餘佛不共法　大自在而坐{83}[94]
一切善皆集　福智以資糧
圓月在星宿　遍滿而圍遶{84}[95]

---

[16] 汝不思思者 (*tvam acintyo 'si* Skt., *khyod ni ... bsam mi khyab* T) : 如汝思思者 Taishō

[17] 禮 (*namo* Skt., *phyag 'tshal* T) : 體 Taishō

[18] 渡 : 度 CAT

則以佛日手　　以寶光無垢
灌頂於長子　　普遍皆令灌{85}[96]
彼住大瑜伽　　皆見以天眼
無明攪擾世[19]　　惡習苦怖畏{86}[97]
狀如金光色　　從彼瑜伽光
彼無知所覆　　得開無明門{87}[98]
以福智感招　　彼獲無執定[20]
隨緣而圓寂　　心得皆變化{88}[99]
諸法無自性　　自性於境界
菩薩王妙見　　法身妙無垢{89}[100]
皆以無垢身　　安住於智海
即作眾生利　　如巧摩尼珠{90}[101]
一切瑜伽者　　大瑜伽自在
佛影皆變化　　遍滿而流出{91}
或有八臂者　　三目熾盛身
彼皆瑜伽王　　普遍而流出{92}
皆以慈悲手[21]　　勝喜執持弓
射以般若箭　　皆斷細無明{93}
以大力昇進　　執持智慧棒
一切無明轂[22]　　普遍皆碎壞{94}
強力諸有情　　金剛熾盛身
調伏有情故　　則為金剛手{95}
自為作業者　　示現種種果

[19] 世 (*'jig rten rams* T) : 出 CAT
[20] 定 (*mya ṅan 'das pa* T) : 受 CAT
[21] 手 : 法 CAT
[22] 轂 : 殼 CAT

教誡[23]如教理　變為平等王{96}
飢渴猛熾身　能施諸飲食
常患諸疾者　則為善醫王{97}
魔王於營從　魔女於莊嚴
菩薩作親友　能施菩提場{98}
猶[24]如日月形　彼光皆悅意
流出如電光　照曜俱胝剎{99}
由以一燈故　遍照皆得然
若一燈滅盡　一切皆隨盡{100}
如是異熟佛　示現種種光
一化現涅槃　餘佛示歸寂{101}
一亦無滅度　日光豈作暗
常現於出沒　示現剎土[25]海{102}
於無智暗世　能淨智慧眼
往於俱胝剎　矜愍化[26]有情{103}
彼皆不疲倦　由彼大慈甲
一切於神足　瑜伽皆彼岸{104}
皆觀時非時　令彼得流轉
剛[27]強於諂曲　暫時而棄捨{105}
無量調有情　頓作令清淨
無量佛變化　頓時得暫變{106}
於三界海中　而擲調伏網
舒展妙法網　普遍令成熟{107}

[23] 誡 : 誠 CAT
[24] 猶 : 由 Taishō
[25] 土 : 上 CAT
[26] 化 : 諸 CAT
[27] 剛 : 則 CAT

則以調伏網　普遍令成熟
普遍覺悟[28]出　於中漂流者{108}
則如千有情　普遍令度已
度已令覺悟　妙法不生疑{109}
世尊妙法鈴　普遍令得聞
由此振聲故　除落煩惱塵{110}
增上無明人　令淨於一時
以日光明威　破壞眾翳瞙[29]{111}
隨從暗煩惱　及餘罪身者
令彼作利益　積漸令清淨{112}
彼彼人現化　安住如水月
煩惱攪擾心　不見於如來{113}<84>[51]
如餓鬼於海　普遍見枯竭
如是少福者　無佛作分別{114}<85>[52]
有情少福者　如來云何作
如於生盲手　安以最勝寶{115}<86>[53]
云何而能見　無上之法身
俱胝日光身[30]　光網以圍遶{116}
諸天以少善　不能而得見
上次於大天　云何而得見{117}
彼色不能見　諸仙離煩惱
天修羅梵等　云何餘少慧{118}
然以佛威力　清淨自心故
能見如是類　獲得一切盛{119}
有情福端嚴　佛住彼人前

[28] 覺悟：舉出 Taishō
[29] 瞙：瞑 CAT
[30] 身：形 CAT

光明照耀身　三十二勝相{120}[54]
彼如是丈夫[31]　當見如大海
不經於多時　即得智如海{121}
世尊彼[32]色身　安住於多劫
能調可調利　趣於戒種類{122}[55]
廣壽大瑜伽　少壽何因故
多人俱胝餘　示現增減壽{123}
無量俱胝劫　以命命增長
因緣皆無盡　獲得無盡果{124}
若有相應顯此理　唯身以慧作分析[33]
彼人生於淨蓮花　聞法所說無量壽{125}

[31] 丈夫：大天 CAT
[32] 彼：被 CAT
[33] 析：折 CAT

Taishō 1675 讚法界頌

聖龍樹菩薩造

西天北印度烏填曩國帝釋宮寺三藏傳法大師賜紫沙門臣施護奉詔譯

歸命十方佛　法身及報化
願共諸眾生　速成法界性 (1)<1>
輪迴三惡道　法界理凝然
本來常清淨　諸相不能遷 (2)<2>
寂靜如虛空　處處悉周遍
體皆離彼此　非深復非淺 (3)
乳未轉變時　酥醍醐不見
煩惱未伏除　法界無由顯 (4)<3>
如酥處乳中　酥本妙光瑩
法界煩惱覆　圓滿體清淨 (5)<4>
如燈被障礙　非能照餘物
無明恒覆心　法界非明了 (6)<5>
如燈離障礙　處處物能照 (7ab)<6>
煩惱破壞時　真如恒顯現 (7cd)<7>
初中及最後　二障不能擾 (8ab)<8>
如淨瑠璃珠　恒時光照曜 (8cd)<9ab>
光明物所障　被障明非見 (9ab)<9cd>
法界煩惱覆　真如理難顯 (9cd)<10ab>
圓寂體光潔　輪迴不能染 (10ab)<10cd>
勤求趣法界　輪迴非能揜[1] (10cd)<11>

---

[1] 揜 : 掩 CAT

如米糠纏裹　穀體米非無
煩惱覆真如　真如煩惱有 (11)<12>
如穀去其糠　米體自然見
若離煩惱糠　法界理方顯 (12)<13>
妄執[2]有世間　芭蕉終無實
法界非世間　亦非虛妄見 (13)<14>
如人飲甘露　熱惱悉皆除
若證法界性　煩惱熱皆棄 (14)
滅除煩惱焰　法界甘露現
一切有情中　高下皆平等 (15)<15>
體實果不生　執種果非有
智慧出生時　有為非法界 (16)<16>
法界本無處　究竟方可證 (17ab)<17ab>
清淨恒光潔　日月皆瑩淨(17c)<18c>,(17d)<18a>
法界無垢染　如龍夜雨塵
況似羅睺面　光明恒燦然 (18)<18b-d>
譬如火浣布　處火能離染
垢去布猶存　光明轉瑩淨 (19)<20>
貪愛令心染　虛妄有輪迴 (20a)<21b>
亦如火浣布　真空妄非有 (20b-d)
三毒生死本　智慧火能燒
法界體常有　朗然恒照曜 (21)<21cd>
煩惱染稱垢　世尊恒所宣 (22ab)<22bc>
垢滅真如顯　如汲地中泉 (22cd)<23ab>
法界體無垢　根隨能覆藏 (2ab)
若除煩惱盡　瑩淨叵難量 (23cd)<23cd>

[2] 執 (*kriyate* Skt.) : 報 CAT

法界本無我　二形及女男
體無虛妄執　何處更思惟 (24)<24>
法界離憎愛　根塵境本無
虛妄執[3]為因　差別從此生 (25)<25>
真空非苦惱　貪愛苦惱因 (26a)<26a>
耽染由妄想　三界乃輪迴 (26c-d)
懷孕在於腹　嬰子未言見
二障覆真如　法界不能證 (27)<27>
種種生疑慮　見慢及恚癡
妄計有真實　真實計非有 (28)
兔角體非有　妄執令真實
法界離妄執　妄執真非有 (29)<30>
如色必破壞　微塵猶可知
法界非破壞　三時不能得 (30)<31>
有生還有滅　榮辱亦皆隨
法界非生滅　云何言所知 (31)<32>
兔角本非有　三世猶可思
真空非兔角　思慮不能知 (32)<33ab>
真空稱善逝　色相悉皆亡
應化隨緣有　修因離執非 (33)<33cd>
圓通如日月　水現影皆同
色聲雙泯絕　差別云何有 (34)<34>
三世可尋思　生緣時決定
若悟己身法　己身云何有 (35)<35>
如水居熱際　處熱覺悟非
寒際理亦然　圓通皆如是 (36)<36>

[3] 執 (妄執 25a, Ch2) : 報 CAT

心恒煩惱覆　迷惑不能了
若離煩惱纏　覺悟而非有 (37)<37>
如眼觀諸色　離障能照曜
真空理亦然　照曜離生滅 (38)<38>
耳識聞於聲　離妄及分別
法界性亦然　分別妄非有 (39)<39>
鼻能嗅諸香　妄執性非有
色相二俱亡　真空亦如是 (40)<40>
舌根自性空　味界恒遠離
識空體亦然　法界理如是 (41)<41>
身根自性淨　冷煖觸非有
法界理亦然　觸處常遠離 (42)<42>
意緣法稱最　自性恒遠離
諸法性本空　圓通理如是 (43)<43>
見聞及覺知　相應法亦空
了絕諸妄想　見聞理亦非 (44)<44>
根塵起妄執　清淨體源無
迷執有根塵　根塵理非有 (45)<45>
世間並出世　空性本無差
我法由迷起　遍計自輪迴 (46)<46>
法界理清淨　貪瞋癡本無
迷悟從心起　三毒法假名 (47)<47>
迷執自纏縛　了達假名智 (48ab)<48>
菩提非近遠　三世理非有 (48cd)<49a-c>
煩惱籠迷執　世尊經所宣 (49ab)<49d, 50a>
智生惑染滅　妄執勿相纏 (49cd)

去來執最勝	體空猶可思	
菩提非妄執	正證[4]亦知非	(50)<51>
水乳同一處	鵝飲乳非雜	(51ab)<52>
生空煩惱離	二障亦非雜	(51cd)<53>
妄執我非無	了達本非有	(52ab)<54>
涅盤[5]清淨理	二我俱非立	(52cd)<55>
三檀齊修施	尸羅離過非	
忍因端正果	精進勇懃依	(53)<56, 57a>
靜慮令心止	般若用無疑	
願兼方便力	安住勝菩提	(54)<57c-d, 58a>
菩提難妄執[6]	眞空生滅無	
了達空本性	二[7]相亦非有	(55)<59>
乳糖離甘蔗	離蔗糖非有	
三乘趣菩提	離種體非有	(56)<60, 61, 62>
守護稻穀種	芽莖必得生	
守護菩提種	菩提從此起	(57)<63>
譬如於黑月	光明未能見	
有情煩惱纏	真如未明顯	(58)<64>
月初光雖有	漸漸而增長	
初地證菩提	菩提未圓滿	(59)<65>
十五月圓滿	處處光皎潔	
解脫顯法身	法身理無缺	(60)<66>
染污意相應	纏縛俱生滅	
解脫一切障	三世悟非有	(61)

[4] 證 (*parijñayā* Skt., *rig gyur pa* T)：登 CAT

[5] 涅盤 ：涅槃 CAT

[6] 執 (妄執 25a, Ch2)：報 CAT

[7] 二 (*byaṅ chub sems dpa' ma byuṅ bar | chos kyi sku ni 'byuṅ ma yin* T)：一 CAT

初大僧祇滿　三檀普遍修
斷除分別障　歡喜智難儔 (62)<68>
三業悞兼犯　防非重及輕
尸羅圓滿戒　離垢獨標名 (63)<69>
二障恒時染　俱空慧刀除
發光能照曜　破滅漸無餘 (64)<70>
遠離根隨染　漸增焰慧威
菩提稱最勝　燒照轉光輝 (65)<71>
真俗稱二智　相應互起違
合令無所礙　難勝事恒時 (66)<72>
十二緣生智　巡環理趣全
甚深稱最勝　般若現於前 (67)<73>
世俗二乘行　久修道已明
相無功用滿　最後稱遠行 (68)<74>
智用[8]無分別　恒時任運成
眾魔降退散　不動獨彰名 (69)<75>
善慧名無礙　十方演法希
身雲甘露雨　應物最堪依 (70)<76>
眾德猶如水　虛空喻似身
重龕皆蔽塞　大法智稱雲 (71)<77>
審諦輪迴事　孰[9]能免業牽 (72ab)<79>
要知無苦惱　淨土勿相纏 (72cd)
歸命佛真子　位登智慧雲
細微皆斷盡　超苦離諸塵 (73)<81>
灌頂諸光照　根塵普遍身
金剛寂大定　眾苦勿相親 (74)

---

8 用 (智用 79a, Ch2) : 界 CAT

9 孰 (*kas* Skt., *gaṅ gis* T) : 熟 CAT

大寶花王座　俱胝眾妙成
莊嚴皆普遍　功德實難思 (75cd)<83>[93]
十力[10]兼無畏　三身四智圓
六通恒自在　應物化機緣 (76)[94]
照曜如圓月　恒時焰熾燃
十方無不遍　燦爛轉光鮮 (77)[95]
永絕緣生染　恒時處涅盤
菩提稱最勝　化益物情歡 (78)[99]
智用深如海　隨機現應身
水清來月影　處處度迷津 (79)[101]
況似頗胝寶　隨緣現影同
物情根有感　周普事無窮 (80)<84>[51]
餓鬼恒飢渴　不能見水泉
眾生無少信　宿業自縈纏 (81)<85>[52]
化現身諸相　光明皆燦然
佛雖恒在世　不覩宿無緣 (82)<86>[53]
曉了塵沙界　根隨染久無
二空殊勝智　妙用化童愚 (83)
清淨絕諸垢　自他受用身
恒居色究竟　利益五乘人 (84)
救護眾生苦　俱胝壽命長
二嚴無有盡　功德叵難量 (85)[55]
佛演一乘法　隨機悟淺深
蓮花無垢染　玉本絕瑕侵 (86)
少分而稱讚　廣宣理趣玄
願將諸功德　普利施人天 (87)

---

[10] 力 (*stobs* T) : 方 CAT

Taishō 2896 示所犯者瑜伽法鏡經

次地藏菩薩讚歎法身觀行品

□□□□□□□　□住智慧大□□
□□□□□在情　喻如意珠無價寶 x+1{90}[101]
一切諸法禪觀中　是大相應觀行主{91ab}
若得最勝相應法　於瑜伽中無與等 x+2
或現梵釋四天王　或作外道大仙眾
或復變化作佛身　普遍法界能出現 x+3{91cd}
或現八臂菩薩等　或現三目光焰盛
彼得瑜伽自在者　能作世間種種身 x+4{92}
能擐慈悲大甲冑　執持歡喜以為弓
巧射智慧善法箭　破彼無明微細中 x+5{93}
具大勢力能速疾　執持智慧堅鐵杵
摧彼無明煩惱轂　普遍碎盡無有餘 x+6{94}
一切力士中最尊　復執金剛火焰杵
為欲調伏眾生故　即現金剛可畏身 x+7{95}
或復現作真金色　光明眾寶自莊嚴
為救貧窮眾生故　即現轉輪聖王身 x+8
若行微妙眾善業　能受種種勝樂果
若能如法教訓人　於彼平等無異見 x+9{96}
於彼飢渴熱惱者　為作種種美飲食
若在疾病苦惱中　現作醫王能救療 x+10{97}
於彼盲冥無智者　為作清淨智慧眼
能行百億佛刹中　慈心調伏眾生故 x+11{103}
不患劬勞辭疲倦　久習慈悲以為體
一切神足自在力　證得瑜伽登彼岸 x+12{104}

不顧好惡慈悲時　一切時中常能度
諂曲鬪諍最惡處　終不暫時起捨心 x+13{105}
容儀晈然如日月　光明隨念應時發
迅疾速現如電光　照彼俱胝諸佛刹 x+14
調伏無量眾生類　平等一時使清淨
普能變化諸佛身　一念之間悉皆現 x+15{106}
三界深廣如大海　普遍澇漉諸有情
巧能張彼善法網　將入調伏佛法城 x+16{107}
由彼調伏網力故　遍能救漉諸眾生
隨所救接得濟者　安置法岸無暫停 x+17{108}
已度有情一切眾　猶如大海水中沙
出已即便示正道　佛法中勝勿須疑 x+18 {109}
佛能執彼法鈴鐸　遍令一切普知聞
以彼振鈴傳法力　煩惱如海咸銷[1]盡 x+19{110}
譬如日光明相現　黑暗障目並蠲除
令彼愚癡無智人　煩惱銷[2]滅慧光淨 x+20{111}
無明煩惱弊其目　一切雜染並隨行
為欲利益眾生故　次第咸令獲清淨 x+21{112}
隨諸眾生示神變　猶如明月水中現
邪智生盲惡眾生　佛對面前而不現 x+22{113}<84>[51]
譬如餓鬼臨大海　盡見海水皆枯竭
如是薄德惡眾生　口常說言無有佛 x+23{114}<85>[52]
此等薄德有情類　諸佛如來不能救
譬如生盲無目人　明珠對前而不見 x+24{115}<86>[53]
誰能有力令觀彼　無垢清淨妙法身
譬如百億日光明　焰網相覆莫能見 x+25{116}

---

[1] 銷 (除落 Ch1) em. : 鎖 Taishō
[2] 銷 (破壞 Ch1) em. : 鎖 Taishō

喻如少福諸天子　下界凡人猶不見
何況自在大天身　豈諸凡愚而得見 x+26{117}
於彼自在天色像　五通仙人尚不見
何況非天八部神　及惡眾生而能見 x+27{118}
要由承佛神力故　能與一切眾生樂
瑜伽觀者淨其心　彼人聰惠即能見 x+28{119}
若有福德眾生者　常感諸佛在其前
圓光圍繞共莊嚴　復具三十二相好 x+29{120}[54]
若知如是大精進　能見智惠深廣海
此等眾生當不久　功德廣大亦如海 x+30{121}
若能聽此妙伽他　自身修行及得見
捨命生大蓮華中　諸佛說法而能聽 x+31{125}

爾時地藏菩薩摩訶薩。說此頌已。頂禮佛足。還復本坐。爾時世尊。告地藏菩薩摩訶薩言。善哉善哉。善男子。汝能善說是妙伽他。若有人能受持讀誦繫念思惟。是人即得一功諸佛無等法藏。亦得不忘諸佛智慧如來祕密藏。故不久於三界中。即得解脫。既自解脫。亦令一切眾生而得解脫。能令聽者依我教行。說此語時。無量天人。入一乘道。復有無量他方菩薩。證得究竟不退轉位。

Appendix

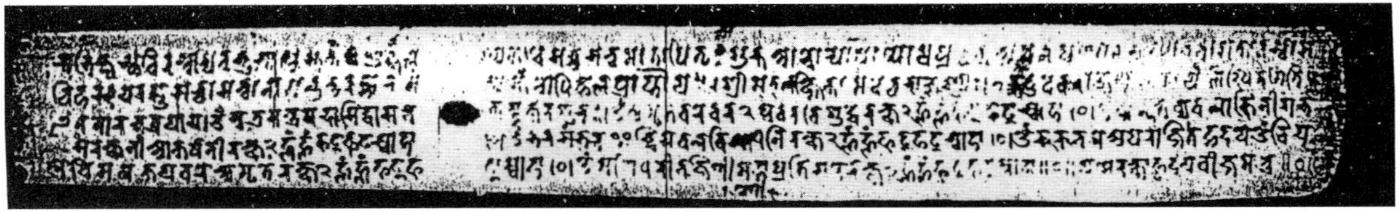

0b of three other folios

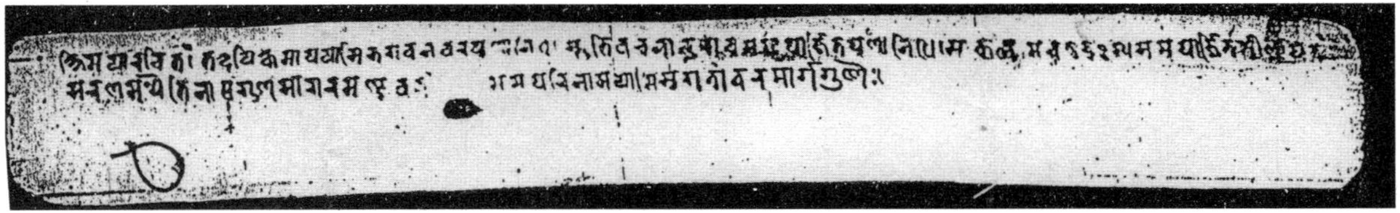

3a of three other folios

Diplomatic Edition of Some Unknown Text(s) which bear(s) a Title *Pañcarakṣāhṛdayabīja-mantra*[1] according to Luo Zhao's Catalogue

3a[2]

3a1 (kya)bhikṣusthavira āryadattasya pustakaṃ .. .. .. le⊙khyakaś ca sarvasatvamātāpitṛ{{m*}} guru ācāryopadhyāyapū(rvakāṇā) anena puṇyena (sukhā va vāgakān svāsa)
3a2 vihara(da$^{?}$)paraṅgu sarvāsatvānām anuttarajñānasa⊙myaksaṃbodhiphalaprāpto yam* | śrīmat* lakṣmikāmadevarājaśrīma(t*){{d}}rudradevarāja .. .. .. yaṃ likhitam iti ||
3a3 namo ratnatrayāya | oṃ atra mantrapadāḥ siddhā sarva⊙karmakara śucaḥ | (oṃ a)mṛtavare vara 2 pravaraviśuddhe rakṣa 2 hūṃ hūṃ phaṭ* phaṭ* svāhā | o | (oṃ am)ṛtavyavalokinī garbha
3a4 saṃrakṣanī ākarṣanī rakṣa 2 hūṃ hūṃ phaṭ* phaṭ* svāhā ⊙ | o | oṃ bhara saṃbhara indriyabalavi{{..}}dhani rakṣa 2 hūṃ hūṃ phaṭ* phaṭ* svāhā | o | oṃ ruru cale aparājitahṛdaya oṃ vipu
5+5 **3a5** le vimale jayavare amṛte rakṣa 2 hūṃ hūṃ phaṭ* pha⊙ṭ* svāhā | o | oṃ ma(ṇ)idharī vajriṇī ma‸‹ṇī›pratisare rakṣa 2 hūṃ hūṃ pha(ṭ* phaṭ*) svāhā || o || pañcarakṣāhṛdayabījamantra || o ||

3b

3b1 namo vāgīśvarāya | ā bodheḥ śaraṇaṃ yāmi buddhaṃ dharmaṃ gaṇottamaṃ bodhau cittaṃ kṛtyam eṣaḥ svaparārthaprasiddhaye 3 || deśanā sarvapāpānāṃ puṇyānāñ cānumodanāṃ | kṛtopavāsaṃ cari
3b2 ṣyāmi | āryāṣṭāṅgikaṃ poṣadhaṃ 3 | sagaṃnvāharantu (ā)⊙(cārya) aham evannāmā | imām velām upādāya | yācar-

---

[1] Cf. 3a5.

[2] The leaves are ordered according to the context, not the pagination.

ya(jirā)gāminī (pattaja) śvaḥ sūryodayāt* | atrāntare satva
3b3 prāṇivadhāt* | parasvaharaṇāt* abrahmacaryāt* | ⊙ (vāg)bhedāt* | anṛtāt* | madopajanāt* | vikālāśanāt* | mālā .. .. (gītalalitāt* | ucca)śayanāt* mahāśa
3b4 yanāt* | adyāhaṃ virat* | × × × × × × karomy arhan* | vṛttaṃ guṇair aṣṭabhi bhūṣitaṃ | 2 | itara me śīlasamvarasamādā(nam | cittālaṃkarā) × × × pariṣkārāya | yogasaṃmbhā

1a

1a1 rāya | uttamārthasya buddhatvasya prāptaye sparṣaṇatāyāstu || utpādayāmye varabodhicittam* | nimantrayāmye ahu sarvasatvām* | iṣṭāṃ cariṣye varabodhicayaritrām* | buddho bhaveyañ jaga
1a2 to´ hitāya || o || ~ namo mañjughoṣāya | suravara⊙ratnamaulimaṇicumbitapādayugaṃ | daśadigaratnatejaguṇasya ganamañjuvaraṃ | śaradaśaśaṃkavarṇṇaḥ dhavalorjvalateja
1a3 × × vapuṃ | praṇamatha vigatamohavāgīśvaram amara⊙gurūṃ | pravarasugandhupuṣpanīlotpalavāmakaraṃ || suratavilāsarāganavayauvanabālatanuṃ | {śa} | daśadigaranta
below 4+41a **1a4** × {ntta}kīrttiguṇajñānasamādhipadaṃ | praṇamatha divya⊙rūpavāgīśvaram ama‹ra›guruṃ || prahaśitadivyakāntivadanottaratejavapum* | nayanaviśālanetranīlotpalapatranibhaṃ

1b

above 1+1 **1 b 1** muditamanopaharṣaśarakāntiśarīradharaṃ | nayanamanoharāya vāgī‹śva›ram amaragurum* | suratavilāsahāsasurasundaridivyarutaiḥ | malayamahīdharāya giriramyasurānilayaiḥ |
1b2 vividhavicitrapuṣpasadabhāgapraharṣatanum* | praṇama⊙tha puṇyakāyavāgīśvaram amaraguru | tribhavanam ekabandhusugatāt*majajeṣṭatanum* | guṇaśatapuṇyakīrttivaranaupu
1b3 rarha{ra}radharam* | tava smaṇābhimantrapratilābha-

samādhi⊙sukhaṃ || praṇamatha śuddhakāyavāgīśvaram amaraṃ guru | divi bhuvi jñānaraśmipariśobhitabālatanum* | vidham{{i}}ha

4+4 **1b4** kleśajāla hṛdi candram ivāpra{{..}}ˇ‹ti›mam* | jagad i‹da› kṛcchraprāpta⊙dakacandrasvabhāvanibhaṃ | praṇamatha jñānakāyavāgīśvaram ama‹ragurum*› khacitamayūkhajvālam upaśobhitadivyatanuṃ ||

0a

1+1 **0a1** suvimalaśuddhakāyahimavantasvabhāvanibhaṃ pravarasvarūpakāya satik{r}āmalabā(la)tanuṃ | praṇamatha vādisiṃhavāgīśvaraˇ‹m amaragurum› sitasatapadmarāgasuvirājitagātrani

0a2 bhaṃ | divi bhuvi ghuṣṭakīrttikamalāsanasita⊙vapuṣaṃ | pravarapracaṇḍabhīmabhayabhairavanāśakaraṃ || ṣraṇamatha divyakāyavāgīśvaram amaragurum* | saga

0a3 ṇasvabhāvabhāvabhayapāpavināśakaraṃ | tri⊙vidham anantaduḥkhagatisadmavināsakaraṃ | abhimatasiddhahetuphalaprāptaguṇe racitaṃ || praṇamatha divya

0a4 kāntivāgīśvaram amaraguruṃ || tribhavamahogha⊙tīrṇṇaguṇasāgarapuṇyanidhiṃ || janapravareṇa mantastutinetraguṇe racitaṃ || tad api ja{śa}ṣa yo pi gurubha

0b

0b1 kti mayā racitaṃ | tad api kṣamāpayāsi bhagavana varapuṇyanidha | stutivacanārṇṇa{ga}va(sa) mayārjitapuṇyaṃ nidhi | sakalam a(vatu) duḥkhasamayārjitatīrṇṇāyataṃ

0b2 saraṇam upaitināthaguṇasāgaramañjuvaraṃ ⊙ mama parināmayāmi sugatāṃ varamārgaguṇaiḥ |

Pāda Index

a

akampyā mārakiṅkaraiḥ 75d
agnimadhye yathā kṣiptaṃ 20c
agniśaucaṃ yathā vastraṃ 20a
acintyo vāsanād muktaś 79a
ajñānaṃ sphorayanti te 53d
atidurbhāṣitaṃ kṛtam 59b
atraiva kleśapañjare 49d
advayaṃ yogināṃ padam 55d
adhimuktidṛḍhaṃ yasya 67a
anābhogavaśiprāptaḥ 75c
anityaduḥkhaśūnyeti 26a
anivartyam bhave bhave 67d
anutpannāniruddhās te 38c
anekaratnapattrābhaṃ 83a
anekaiḥ padmakoṭībhiḥ 83c
apratiṣṭhitavijñānaṃ 41c
apramāṇāndhakārasya 70c
abhranīhāradhūmena 18c
amṛtaṃ sarvadehinām 15d
arūpam anidarśanam 40b
arhatpratyekabuddhānām 62c
avabhāsāḥ sunirmalāḥ 38b
avisaṃvādakaṃ dhruvam 35b
asmiṃ kalevare sarvaṃ 48a
ahaṃmamavikalpo hi 28c
ahaṃ mameti vā grāho 54a

ā

ākāśam iva nirmalam

77b
ātmagrāheṇa saṃsāraḥ
46c
ādimadhyāntakalyāṇam
35a
ādimadhyāntanirmalaḥ
8d
ābhā tasya na rājate
9d
āvṛtaṃ kleśajālena
37a
āvṛtau pañcabhir malaiḥ
18b, 19b
āśrayaḥ sarvadharmāṇāṃ
78a
āśrayasya parāvṛttir
78c
āsanaṃ sampratiṣṭhati
82d

u

uktaṃ ca sūtravargeṣu
50a
uttīrṇaṃ bhavasāgarāt
82b
utpattir bhūtabhautikāt
28b
utpattis tatra jāyate
61d, 62d
utpādayati tac cittam
67c
utpādavyayagambhīrā
73c
udakaṃ ca tathā sthitam
52d
upamā kriyate loke
14a
upāyasahitā prajñā
58a
ubhau kalpitalakṣaṇau
33b
uṣṇam ity abhidhīyate
36b

e

ekasya sambhavo nāsti
32c
etat tattvasya lakṣaṇam
45d
evaṃ niṣpannalakṣaṇam
44d
evaṃ prabhāsvaraṃ cittaṃ
19a, 21a
evaṃ hi kleśasañchanno
10a
evaṃ hi kleśasammiśraṃ
53a
evaṃ hi sarvabījeṣu
16a
evaṃ hy asāre saṃsāre
15a

au

auddhatyavicikitsayā
19d

k

kaḥ prājñaḥ pratipatsyate
16d
kathaṃ bālair vikalpyate
32d
katham ātmeti kalpyate
24d, 35d
kadalyā nāsti sāratā

14b
kalpayanti dvayaṃ bālā 55c
kalpitaṃ naiva vidyate 30d
kalpyakalpanavarjitam 43b
kalpyamānaṃ na vidyate 30b
kas tvā vijñātum arhati 79d
kāmavyāpādamiddhena 19c
kāyaṃ jñānamayaṃ rāmyam 77a
kṛṣṇāśrayaparāvṛttiḥ 68a
krameṇa samudānītā 81a
krīḍate raśmijālena 74a
kleśair antaritaṃ jñānaṃ 23c
kleśair malinasattvānāṃ 84c
kṣīraṃ pibanti haṃsā hi 52c
kṣīram ekatra bhājane 52b

g

guḍaśarkarakhaṇḍānām 61c
gotre asati vyāyāmaḥ 11c
gotre ca sati vyāyāmo 11a
goviṣāṇaṃ na vidyate 31b
grīṣmakāle yathā vāri 36a

gh

ghṛtadravyaṃ sunirmalam 4b
ghrāṇaṃ gandhāśritaṃ ghrā-ṇi 40a
ghrāṇavijñānatathatā 40c

c

cakravyūhaiḥ samantataḥ 74b
cakṣuḥ pratītya rūpaṃ ca 38a
cakṣuḥ śrotraṃ ca ghrāṇaṃ ca 45a
caturṇāṃ hi vikalpānām 28a
caryāphalaparigrahaḥ 78b
cittaṃ vijñaptayas trayaḥ 39b
cittanidhyaptayas trayaḥ 26b
cittam ity abhidhīyate 37b
cittam eva dvidhā dṛṣṭaṃ 46a
cintyaḥ saṃsāravāsanaḥ 79b

cchidrībhavati tad ghaṭam 6b

j

jātarūpanidarśanāt 11b
jātyandhasya haste yathā[1] 86c
jihvā kāyo manas tathā 45b
jihvā svabhāvaśūnyā hi 41a
jñānam ajñānam eva ca 48b
jñānam ekatra bhājane 53b
jñānāgninā malaṃ dagdhaṃ 21c
jñānārciṣaiḥ parivṛtā 71c

t

tat phalaṃ pratibhāsate 13b
tathā kleśaghaṭastho hi 5c
tathāgrayānādhimuktānāṃ 64c
tathā niṣṭhāgatābhūmyāṃ 66c
tathā niṣpannalakṣaṇam 34d
tathābhāti sunirmalam 23d
tathā bhūmipraviṣṭānāṃ 65c
tathā viśodhitāḥ kleśā 4c
tathāśrayādhimuktānāṃ 63c
tathā hi kleśanirmukto 13c
tathā hi kleśasañchannaṃ 27c
tathā hi kleśasañchanno 12c
tathā hi kleśasammiśro 3c
tathā hi sarvadharmeṣu 30c
tathaivājñānadagdhānāṃ 85c
tadā tasyāvabodhena 68c
tad eva kleśāpagamād 37c
tad eva śītakāleṣu 36c
tasya kiṃ kalpyate budhaiḥ 31d
tasya bodhāya buddhatvaṃ 47c
tiṣṭhate bālacandravat 84b
tisṛṇām api bodhīnāṃ 73a
tena tena hi pārśvena 6c

[1] The latter part of this *pāda*, *ndhasya haste yathā*, is missing in CE and reconstructed according to T and Ch1.

trilokāt tīrṇapaṅkaughair 74c
tvam acintyo 'si sarveṣāṃ 79c

d

daśabhiś ca balair bālas 84a
durjayānāṃ hi kleśānāṃ 72c
duṣkarair vividhair dānaiḥ 56a
dūraṅgamā iti smṛtā 74d
dṛśyate candravigraham 64b
dṛśyate pratibimbaṃ hi 34c
dṛśyate buddhavigraham 64d
dṛṣṭā vṛddhiḥ kṣaṇe kṣaṇe 65b, d
dṛṣṭe viṣayanairātmye 54c
dveṣamohakṣayaś ca yat 47b

dh

dharmakāyaḥ prabhāsate 13d
dharmakāyaḥ sa eva hi 2d
dharmakāyo 'bhidhīyate 78d
dharmakāyo hi jāyate 66d
dharmatattvaṃ na dṛśyate 27d
dharmadeśena sāṅkathyair 76c
dharmadhātuṃ prajānatha 38d
dharmadhātuṃ vadāmy aham 42d
dharmadhātuḥ sunirmalaḥ 4d, 10b
dharmadhātur alakṣaṇaḥ 39d
dharmadhātur na cotpanno 8a
dharmadhātur na dṛśyate 3d
dharmadhātur na bhāsate 5d
dharmadhātur yato nātmā 24a
dharmadhātur vikalpyate 40d
dharmadhātur vibhāvyate 43d
dharmadhātusvabhāvatā 41d
dharmadhāto namas tubhyaṃ 1a
dharmameghā samantataḥ 77d
dharmameghena jñānena 81c
dharmāṇāṃ niḥsvabhāvatā 26d
dharmāṇāṃ niḥsvabhāvatvaṃ

43c
dharmāṇām āśrayo mataḥ
17b
dharmān vijānate yogī
44c
dhātupuṣṭiś caturvidhā
58d
dhātupuṣṭir iyaṃ tridhā
56d
dhyānānāṃ ca vicitratā
72b
dhyāne cittaṃ pracāritam
57b

n

na kiñcid avabhāsate
5b
na gatā nāpi vāgatā
49b
na ca strīnṛnapuṃsakaḥ
24b
na dagdhaṃ tat prabhāsva-
ram
21d
na dṛśyate dṛśyate caiva
49c
na dhānyaṃ tat phalaṃ ma-
tam
12b
na niruddhaḥ kadācana
8b
na paśyati tathāgatam
84d
na bodher dūraṃ sañjñī syān
51a
na sāsannā ca sañjñinaḥ
51b
nāmasañjñānimittajaḥ
28d
nāsau buddheti kalpyate
12d
nāsau bhrājati saṃsāre
10c
nirābhāsam alakṣaṇam
29b
nirodhāt kleśajālasya
70a
nirmalau candrasūryau hi
18a
nirvāṇe tu prabhāsvaraḥ
10d
nirvṛte kleśasāgare
15b

naiva dhātor vināśanam
22d

p

paramā cittanidhyaptir
26c
paramāṃ śāntim āgataḥ
50d
paramāṇurajaḥ kintu
31a
paśyate śṛṇute ghrāti
44a
pāṣāṇakośe sañchannam
9c
pibanti yogino jñānam
53c
pūrṇacandro hi jāyate
66b
pṛthivyantarhitaṃ toyaṃ

23a
prajñādīpavihāreṇa 50c
prajñāyām acalaṃ nityaṃ 57c
praṇidhānaṃ hi buddhānāṃ 29a
praṇidhānair viśodhitā 58b
pratisaṃvitsu sarvāsu 76a
pratītya ca nirudhyate 32b
pratītyotpadyate caiva 32a
pratyayebhyo vinirmuktaṃ 42c
pratyātma tathatā hi tat 46d
pratyātmavedyayogitvād 29c
prabhābhrājavinirmalā 70b
praviṣṭo jñānasāgare 75b

ph

phalaṃ tasyāpi buddhatvam 15c
phalāni tasya sārāṇi 14c

b

badhyate svavikalpena 48c
baleṣu suṣṭhitaṃ jñānaṃ 58c
bījabhūtas tv asau dhātur 17a
bījair vinā phalaṃ nāsti 16c
buddha ity abhidhīyate 37d
buddhatvāspadam āvahet 17d
buddhaputrā mahāyaśāḥ 81b
buddhānāṃ nityadharmatā 29d
buddhe dharme ca nityaśaḥ 67b
buddho nāstīti kalpanā 85d
buddho hi parinirvāti 55a
buddhaiḥ sandhriyamāṇo 'sau 75a
bodhipuṣṭir iyaṃ punaḥ 57d
bodhir na dūre nāsanne 49a
bodhisattvam ajīvaṃ tu 59c

bh

bhakṣyate amṛtopamā 14d
bhagavān kiṃ kariṣyati 86b
bhavabījaṃ nirudhyate 54d
bhinnaṃ bhavati tad ghaṭam 7b

bhūmiḥ sādhumatī smṛtā 76d
bhūmir arciṣmatī matā 71d
bhūmis tv abhimukhībhūtā 73d
bhramanti tribhavālaye 1d

m

madhyamā pratipadyeta 33c
manaḥ pradhānadharmeṣu 43a
manovijñānagamyo 'si 80c
malaṃ dagdhaṃ na vastratā 20d
malābhāve ca yā śuddhiḥ 69c
malinaṃ nityakālaṃ hi 69amalinaṃ rāgajair malaiḥ 21b
malinaṃ vividhair malaiḥ 20b
mahāpadmamayaṃ tasya 82c
mā bodhisattvān tu vandeti 59a
mucyate svaparijñayā 48d
muditety abhidhīyate 68d

y

ya eva dhātuḥ saṃsāre 2a
yathā kṛṣṇacaturdaśyāṃ 64a
yathā candrārkatārāṇāṃ 34a
yathā tiṣṭhati nirmalam 23b
yathā dīpo ghaṭastho hi 5a
yathā pūrvaṃ tathā paścāt 31c
yathābhūtaṃ parijñayā 51d
yathā viśodhitaṃ kṣīraṃ 4a
yathā vaiḍūryaratnaṃ hi 9a
yathā śaśaviṣāṇaṃ hi 30a
yathā śālyāṅkurādīnāṃ 63a
yathā sugatadharmatā 33d
yathā hi kṣīrasammiśraṃ 3a
yathā hi garbho garbhiṇyāṃ 27a
yathā hi tuṣanirmuktaṃ 13a
yathā hi tuṣasañchannaṃ 12a
yathā hi pañcadaśyāṃ vai 66a
yathodakena sammiśraṃ 52a
yathaiva bālacandrasya 65a
yadā prakṣālitaṃ cittam

82a
yadā pretāḥ samantāt tu 85a
yadā samādhivajreṇa 7a
yasya caivaṃvidhānātmā 35c
yasya te aparijñānād 1c
yāvad bāhyo vikalpyate 54b
ye kecid bhāṣitā jinaiḥ 22b
yena yena hi pārśvena 6a
yo 'si yo 'si namo 'stu te 80d

r
rakṣāṃ kurvanti kārṣikāḥ 63b
rakṣāṃ kurvanti nāyakāḥ 63d
rakṣite bodhicitte hi 62a
raśmayas tasya nirgatāḥ 6d
rasadhātur viviktatā 41b
rāgakṣayo hi nirvāṇaṃ 47a
rāgādyair vividhair malaiḥ 69b
rāgāndhavineyārthāya 25c
rāhuvaktrarajādibhiḥ 18d

l
lakṣaṇojjvalakalpikam 83b
loki lokottaraṃ ca yat 46b

v
vigatā tu prabhākarī 70d
vijayā tu sudurjayā 72d
vidyate na ca dṛśyate 27b
vimalety abhidhīyate 69d
viharaty ātmacintakaḥ 50b
vīryaṃ ca sarvadharmeṣu 57a

ś
śaraṇaṃ sarvadehinām 47d
śaśagośṛṅgadṛṣṭāntam 33a
śītam ity abhidhīyate 36d
śīlaiḥ sattvārthasaṅgrahaiḥ 56b
śuklāśrayaparigrahaḥ 68b
śucir nityaśubhālayaḥ 55b
śuddhaḥ sa eva nirvāṇe 2c
śuddhakāyasvabhāvena

42a
śuddhā prabhāsvarā nityaṃ 71a
śuṣkaṃ paśyanti sāgaram 85b
śūnyatāhārakāḥ sūtrā 22a
śūnyaṃ paśyanti dharmatām 81d
śodhyamānaḥ krameṇaivaṃ 17c
śodhyamānaḥ sa eva tu 2b
śramaḥ kevalam iṣyate 11d
śrūyate svavikalpena 39c
śrotraṃ pratītya śabdaṃ ca 39a

ṣ

ṣaḍāyatanaṃ viśuddham 45c
ṣaṇṇāṃ hi viṣayābhāso 51c

s

saṅgajaiḥ parivarjitā 71b
saṅgrahaḥ sarvasampadām 73b
sa tadākāśaparyantaṃ 7c
sattvānām alpapuṇyānāṃ 86a
sattvopakārakṣāntyā ca 56c
sandhārayati buddhānāṃ 77c
sannidhāyātra cintayet 61b, 62b
samantāt parivāritaṃ 83d
samantād avabhāsate 7d
sa yogī pāramīgataḥ 76b
sarpimaṇḍaṃ na dṛśyate 3b
sarvakālaprabhāsvaram 9b
sarvakālam asaṅkliṣṭa 8c
sarvagrāhavinirmuktaḥ 24c
sarvavāgviṣayātītaṃ 80a
sarvavidyākalāśilpa- 72a
sarvasattveṣv avasthita 1b
sarve dharmā hy asaṃsaktāḥ 25a
sarvendriyam agocaram 80b
sarvais taiḥ kleśavyāvṛttir 22c
sādṛśyaṃ jāyate phalam 16b
strīpuṃstvaṃ hi na vidyate 25b
strīpuṃstvaṃ hi pradarśitam 25d
sparśapratyayalakṣaṇam

42b
svaccha udakabhājane 34b
svādate spṛśatīti ca 44b

Bibliography

BRUNNHÖLZL 2007

KARL BRUNNHÖLZL, *In Praise of Dharmadhātu. Nāgārjuna and the Third Karmapa, Rangjung Dorje*. Ithaca: Snow Lion Publication 2007.

CARELLI 1941

MARIO E. CARELLI, *Sekoddeśaṭīkā of Naḍapāda (Nāropā), Being a commentary of the Sekkoddeśa Section of the Kālacakra Tantra, The Sanskrit Text edited for the first time with an introduction in English*. B. Bhattacharyya et al. (eds.), Gaekwad's Oriental Series XC. Baroda: Oriental Institute 1941.

CHOU 1945,

CHOU YI-LIANG, Tantrism in China. In: *Harvard Journal of Asiatic Studies* 8, no. 3 and 4, 1945, 241-332.

ECKEL 2008

MALCOLM DAVID ECKEL, *Bhāviveka and his Opponents*. Harvard Oriental Series 70. Cambridge, Mass: Harvard University Press 2008.

HAYASHIMA 1987

OSAMU HAYASHIMA, Sanhokkaijuko ("讃法界頌"考). In: *Nagasakidaigaku Kyōikugakubu Shakaikagakuronsō* (*長崎大學教育學部社會科學論叢*) 36, 1987, 41-90.

KRASSER 2012

HELMUT KRASSER, Bhāviveka, Dharmakīrti and Kumārila. In: François Voegeli et al (eds.), *Devadattiyam: Johannes Bronkhorst felicitation volume, Worlds of South and Inner Asia* (Welten Süd- und Zentralasiens, Mondes de l'Asie du Sud et de L'Asie central);

5. Bern, Berlin, Bruxelles, Frankfurt am Main, New York, Oxford, Wien: Peter Lang Verlag 2012, 535-594.

LINDTNER 1982
CHRISTIAN LINDTNER, *Nagarjuniana. Studies in the Writings and Philosophy of Nāgārjuna*. Indiske Studier IV. Copenhagen: Akademisk Forlag 1982.

MACDONALD 2005
ANNE MACDONALD, Manuscript Description. In: ERNST STEINKELLNER, HELMUT KRASSER, HORST LASIC (eds.), *Jinendrabuddhi's Viśālāmalavatī Pramāṇasamuccayaṭīkā*, Chapter 1. Part II, (STTAR 1/II) Beijing-Vienna: CTRC-AAS 2005, ix-xxxvi.

MAIR & MEI 1991
VICTOR MAIR & TSU-LIN MEI, The Sanskrit Origins of Recent Style Prosody. In: *Harvard Journal of Asiatic Studies* 51. 2, 1991, 375-470.

MOCHIZUKI 1931-37
SHINKŌ MOCHIZUKI, *Bukkyō daijiten (望月佛教大辭典)*, 6 vols., Kyoto: Sekai Seiten Kankō Kyōkai 1931-37.

MOCHIZUKI 2008
KAIGYOKU MOCHIZUKI, Dol po pa は *Dharmadhatustava* をどのように読んだのか[On the Commentary to the *Dharmadhatustava* by Dol po pa]. In: *The Japanese Association of Indian and Buddhist Studies* 56.2, 2008, 85-91.

PETECH 1984
LUCIANO PETECH, *Mediaeval History of Nepal (c. 750-1482). Serie Orientale Roma* LIV. Roma: Istituto Italiano per il Medio ed Estremo Oriente 1984[2].

SCHMITHAUSEN 1969
LAMBERT SCHMITHAUSEN, *Der Nirvāṇa-Abschnitt in der Viniścayasaṃgrahaṇī der Yogācārabhūmiḥ. Österreichische Akademie der Wissenschaften, Philosophisch-historische Klasse Sitzungsberichte,* 264. 2. *Veröffentlichungen der Kommission für Sprachen und Kulturen Süd- und Ostasiens,* Heft 8. Wien: Hermann Böh-

laus Nachf. Kommissionsverlag der Österreichischen Akademie der Wissenschaften 1969.

SEN 2002
TANSEN SEN, The Revival and Failure of Buddhist Translations during the Song Dynasty. In: *T'oung Pao*, Second Series, 88, Fasc. 1/3, 2002, 27-80.

SEYFORT RUEGG 1971
DAVID SEYFORT RUEGG, Le Dharmadhātustava de Nāgārjuna. In: *Etudes Tibétaines. Dédiées à la Mémore de Marcelle Lalou*. Paris: Librairie d'Amérique et d'Orient 1971, 448-471.

SEYFORT RUEGG 1990
DAVID SEYFORT RUEGG, On the authorship of some works ascribed to Bhāvaviveka/Bhavya. In: D. Seyfort Ruegg & L. Schmithausen (eds.), *Earliest Buddhism and Madhyamaka*. J. Bronkhorst (ed.), *Panels of the VIIth World Sanskrit Conference, Kern Institute, Leiden: August 23-29, 1987, II, Earliest Buddhism and Madhyamaka*. Leiden: Brill 1990, 59-71.

SFERRA & MERZAGORA 2006
FRANCESCO SFERRA & STEFANIA MERZAGORA, *The Sekoddeśaṭīkā by Nāropā (Paramārthasaṃgraha)*. Serie Orientale Roma XCIX. Roma: Istituto Italiano per l'Africa e l'Oriente 2006.

STEINKELLNER 2007
ERNST STEINKELLNER, *Dharmakīrti's Pramāṇaviniścaya, Chapter 1 and 2*: Critically edited by Ernst Steinkellner. (STTAR 2) Beijing-Vienna: CTRC-AAS 2007.

TSUKINOWA 1933
KENYO TSUKINOWA, 竜樹菩薩の讃法界頌と百千頌大集経地藏菩薩請問法身賛と，西藏文の“Dharmadhātustotra”とに就て，竜谷学報 306, 419-444; 307, 516-543.

TSUKINOWA 1934
KENYO TSUKINOWA, 法界讃内容考，竜谷学報 308, 29-51.

YABUKI 1927

KEIKI YABUKI, *Sangaikyō no kenkyū* (三階教之研究), Tokyo: Iwanami Shoten 1927.

ZIMMERMANN 2002

MICHAEL ZIMMERMANN, *A Buddha Within: The Tathāgatagarbhasūtra. The Earliest Exposition of the Buddha-Nature Teaching in India*. Hiroshi Kanno (ed.), *Bibliotheca Philologica et Philosophica Buddhica*, VI. Tokyo: The International Research Institute for Advanced Buddhology, Soka University 2002.

- -

图书在版编目（CIP）数据

赞法界颂:梵文/ 刘震校注. - - 北京 : 中国藏学出版社，2015.4

ISBN 978-7-80253-787-3

Ⅰ. ①赞… Ⅱ. ①刘… Ⅲ. ①古典诗歌-诗集-中国-宋代-梵语 Ⅳ. ①I222

中国版本图书馆CIP数据核字(2015)第066096号

- -

《赞法界颂》 刘震 校注

出版：中国藏学出版社
发行：中国藏学出版社
责任编辑：南加才让
封面设计：李建雄
印刷：北京隆昌伟业印刷有限公司
开本：787×1092 1/16
印张：8.25
印次：2015年4月第1版第1次
印数：700
书号：ISBN 978-7-80253-787-3/I · 149
定价：25.00元